Bird Strike

Bird Strike

The Crash of the Boston Electra

MICHAEL N. KALAFATAS

Brandeis University Press
Waltham, Massachusetts
PUBLISHED BY
UNIVERSITY PRESS OF NEW ENGLAND
HANOVER AND LONDON

Brandeis University Press
Published by University Press of New England
One Court Street, Lebanon NH 03766
www.upne.com

Manufactured in the United States of America
Designed by Katherine B. Kimball
Typeset in Scala by Integrated Publishing Solutions

University Press of New England is a member of the
Green Press Initiative. The paper used in this book
meets their minimum requirement for recycled paper.

Library of Congress Cataloging-in-Publication Data
Kalafatas, Michael N.
Bird strike : the crash of the Boston Electra /
Michael N. Kalafatas.
    p. cm.
Includes bibliographical references.
ISBN 978-1-58465-897-9 (cloth : alk. paper)
1. Aircraft bird strikes—Massachusetts—
Boston.   2. Aircraft accidents—Massachusetts—
Boston.   3. Electra (Turboprop transports)   I. Title.
TL553.525.M4K35   2010
363.12'465—dc22   2010013165

5 4 3 2 1

Across the veil of time,
for the passengers and crew of Eastern Airlines Flight 375,
and for my grandchildren: may they fly in safe skies

The bell-beat of their wings above my head.
—W. B. YEATS, "The Wild Swans at Coole"

Contents

Illustrations follow page 98

Preface: A Clear and Present Danger

I write this on the first anniversary of the so-called miracle on the Hudson, when a brilliant pilot and Lady Luck, with fine teamwork, glided a powerless giant airliner to a safe landing on a great American river, six minutes after takeoff. Captain Chesley B. "Sully" Sullenberger and Lady Luck saved the lives of 155 passengers and crew—better known as loved ones to those who pine for them when away, praying for their safe return.

The miracle on the Hudson should have been an alarm call, awakening us to the danger of catastrophic airliner crashes caused by bird strike. Relying on miracles—the confluence of a pilot with decades of glider experience, a glass-flat river, a fleet of ferry boats at the ready—is not sound transportation safety policy. The event described in this book—the downing of a Lockheed Electra by a flock of 10,000 starlings in 1960—remains, as of this writing, the worst aviation disaster caused by bird strike. In that crash sixty-two people died; ten survived because of the heroism of ordinary citizens, many of them young boys. Its place in history is likely to be supplanted soon by a far worse aviation disaster, for reasons described in this book. Indeed, one could have happened on January 15, 2009.

It is rare that an author can write simultaneously about a historical event that happened half a century ago and a clear and present danger today. The reasons for that danger are many; here are just two. First, the populations of thirteen of the fourteen largest birds found in North America are dramatically on the rise; any one of these birds is capable of shutting down a modern jet engine. Typically these birds fly in flocks—as was the case when Captain Sullenberger's US Airways Flight 1549 struck the flock of Canada geese. Second, in a quiet but dangerous revolution, in one generation the airlines have shifted away from use of jetliners powered by three or four engines to jetliners powered by two engines. It is far easier for birds to disable a plane with two engines than one with four engines. Redundancy in jet engines increases the probability that an aircraft would not be left powerless after a bird strike and can make a safe emergency landing at an airport possible. Part of this book is the amazing story of the crash of the Lockheed Electra, the heroism of citizens, and the greatest rescue mobilization Boston has ever witnessed. The rest of the book explores how we can find a better way to share the skies with the avian life we so longed to be like when we first took to the skies in powered flight at Kitty Hawk.

Bird Strike

1 Appointment in Samarra

What happens when dreams collide?

On June 13, 1923, the first plane touched down on the 1,500-foot cinder runway of tiny Boston Airport, built by the U.S. Army on 189 acres of tidal flats in East Boston. Two decades earlier the Wright brothers had achieved humankind's dream to defy gravity and reach for the sun-split clouds. Amazingly, for thirty-seven years Boston's airport, one of the nation's busiest, did not see a single fatality from a commercial aviation crash. In 1943 the airport was renamed Logan after a distinguished Boston public servant—General Edward Lawrence Logan—who reportedly never flew in an airplane.

On the warm and golden afternoon of October 4, 1960, Logan Airport's innocence came to a ghastly end. As families along Winthrop Harbor sat down to supper and as I arrived at my job of soda jerk in South Boston, across the cheerful blue waters of Boston Harbor from the airport, a Lockheed Electra taking off slammed into a flock of ten thousand starlings and another human dream: one man's determination to bring to the United States all the songbirds that dart across the pages of Shakespeare's plays. That collision of dreams would take sixty-two lives and give rise to some of the greatest heroism Boston has ever witnessed—including the heroism of children.

A Feathered Bullet

A New York drug manufacturer, Eugene Schieffelin, released sixty European starlings into Central Park in 1890, and forty more birds a year later. The experiment was a stunning success: today there are 200 million starlings in North America, here because of a fleeting reference in *Henry IV* to the starling's ability to mimic the human voice.

Like a flight of swallows or an exaltation of larks, a group of starlings has a special name: a murmuration of starlings. The birds mimic whatever they hear—voices, telephones, car alarms, barking dogs, other birds—and their song is a medley of squeaks, clicks, whistles, and other interpretations of the world of sound.

An average starling weighs only 2.82 ounces, about the heft of a cellphone, but in fall and winter starlings swarm together in enormous flocks containing up to a million birds, and they wheel in flight with military precision. Fast-flying and relatively dense, a single starling can be a feathered bullet; a swarm of the birds is a feathered fusillade. After a day's foraging—finding their food on the ground, up to seventy miles away—they splash clean in water, if they can, and return to their roost at sunset. Before Boston's Big Dig, 160,000 would fly at sunset to a favorite roost on the Tobin Bridge, jostling for a spot and murmuring away at evening commuters. Perhaps that's where the birds were bound that fateful fall day in 1960.

On October 4, a half-hour before sunset and before the rise of a blood-red harvest moon, Eastern Airlines Flight 375, a four-engine Lockheed Electra turboprop—bound for Philadelphia; Charlotte, North Carolina; Greenville, South Carolina; and Atlanta, Georgia—rose from Runway 9 with seventy-two souls on board. Among them were fifteen newly-sworn-in marines en route to training at Parris Island, South Carolina; Philadelphians headed home after a shoe convention in Boston; baseball fans on their way to the World Series in Pittsburgh, where the Pirates would play the Yankees (Art Ditmar, born in Winthrop, Massachusetts, would be opening pitcher for the Yanks and would last only a third of an inning); and an engineer with top-secret plans for a new missile system sealed in a specially locked briefcase. Ted Williams, who six days earlier had bade Boston adieu with a home run in his last at bat, was a near miss to be on the flight.

Twenty-seven seconds after it began its takeoff and only seven seconds into the flight, the Lockheed Electra took a fusillade of feathered bullets into three of its four engines. It was a fatal shooting.

Whipped in through air scoops, starlings jammed the jet compressors and blades of the turbines (from *turbo*, the Latin for "whirl"), whose job it was to spin freely—as jet exhaust roared past them—to power the plane's propellers and power and cool its compressors. A turboprop is a hybrid, part jet and part propeller, a design that is still in use, and efficient and economical in regional air traffic. With a turboprop, the jet exhaust doesn't directly drive the plane; instead, the jet exhaust powers the propellers that drive the plane.

In the 1950s, it was my dad's job to grind turbine blades to extremely fine tolerances for GE's J-47 engine, used on the F-86 Sabre Jet—pride of the U.S. Air Force in Korea, with its 14:1 kill ratio over the Russian-built MiG. A slight flaw or disturbance in the balance or free-flow spin of turbine blades could cause a Sabre Jet to vibrate to death at 700 miles per hour—sending it into the Sea of Japan.

Just before the Lockheed Electra was cleared for takeoff in Boston, two Sabre Jets zoomed off from Logan to chase the shouting wind at 45,000 feet. In its initial climb off Runway 9, the Lockheed Electra struck the flock of starlings, estimated at 10,000 to 20,000 birds. The plane's number one engine—the engine on the left wing farthest from the fuselage—shut down, giving off a puff of grey smoke. The Electra could fly on its three other engines, but then two more experienced losses of power. The number two engine—the one on the left wing closest to the fuselage—flashed flame and shut down, and the number four engine—on the right wing farthest from the fuselage—lost power. With no engine power on the left and only partial power on the right, the plane veered sharply to the left in its upward struggle and slowed to stall speed. The left wing then dropped, the nose pitched up, and the plane rolled left into a spin and plunged nearly vertically into Winthrop Harbor.

So caught by surprise were the pilot and copilot that they never uttered a word to the Logan tower. The plane struck the water halfway between the end of Runway 9 and the Winthrop shore, amid pleasure craft anchored 200 yards off the Cottage Park Yacht Club. The impact was so violent the plane burst apart, sending a geyser upward; its tail broke off and hit the water still dry; and all but two passenger seats were ripped from the plane's floor. The main section sank in a few minutes in thirty feet of water; the tail floated and drifted—with a half-dozen bodies visible within—before it too sank a little later. Winthrop residents thought they'd heard a sonic boom.

What followed was the largest rescue mobilization Boston has ever witnessed—exceeding that of the 1942 Cocoanut Grove nightclub fire when 492 people perished and 166 were injured. The response to the plane crash was characterized by spontaneous generosity and heroism offered without a moment's hesitation—and, most touchingly, by boys hardly out of childhood.

As of this writing, a half-century later, the Boston crash of the Electra remains the worst disaster in aviation history caused by bird strike and among the top fifty air disasters in the United States. In the chain of events that led up to the Electra's plunge into Winthrop Harbor, any of twenty links might have been broken—by chance, human prescience, a shift forward or backward of five seconds in takeoff, or a lifting of what seemed to be a curse on the new Lockheed Electra L-188, with four crashes in nineteen months. (It was also the daughter of the Model 10E Electra, the last plane ever flown by Amelia Earhart.) Yet none of the links in the chain of events did break.

One is left to ponder inevitability or fate. One afternoon in 1960, at the soda fountain where I worked, I snagged from a slim bookstand a new edition of John O'Hara's *Appointment in Samarra*, in which the foreword quotes Somerset Maugham's recounting of an Arab legend:

Death Speaks

There was a merchant in Bagdad who sent his servant to market to buy provisions and in a little while the servant came back, white and trembling, and said, Master, just now when I was in the market-place I was jostled by a woman in the crowd and when I turned I saw it was Death that jostled me. She looked at me and made a threatening gesture; now, lend me your horse, and I will ride away from this city and avoid my fate. I will go to Samarra and there Death will not find me. The merchant lent him his horse, and the servant mounted it, and he dug his spurs in its flanks and as fast as the horse could gallop he went. Then the merchant went down to the market-place and he saw me standing in the crowd and he came to me and said, Why did you make a threatening gesture to my servant when you saw him this morning? That was not a threatening gesture, I said, it was only a start of surprise. I was astonished to see him in Bagdad, for I had an appointment with him tonight in Samarra.

2 Crimson Sunset

An inbound pilot barked, "Tower, an Electra just went into the drink."—*Time*, October 17, 1960

A little after 5:15 on the afternoon of Tuesday, October 4, 1960, a small party of family and friends of Frederick Nino Abate, an 18-year-old marine recruit from Quincy, Massachusetts, climbed the stairs to the observation deck at Logan Airport to watch his plane take off. The group consisted of Freddie's mother, father, sister, brother-in-law, friend Jack, and girlfriend, Pat Connelly. They wanted to wave good-bye to Freddie and the other boys headed off to boot camp at Parris Island. The six people in the Abate party were the only people out on the open deck. A light breeze blew out of the southeast as the huge crimson disk of the October sun began its slide to the west behind Boston's low skyline: the stately Custom House, the old twenty-six-story John Hancock Building, and the landmark U.S. Post Office Building, now pouring out into the financial district federal workers done for the day—some of whom owed their jobs to Senator John F. Kennedy, the man they hoped would be elected president in four weeks. This Tuesday had been as stunning an autumn day as New England can muster. A Canadian high-pressure system had revolutionized Boston's weather after an especially rainy September. Indeed, on September 29, Ted Williams's hard-hit home run in his final at bat had to fight its way through heavy, soggy air all the way into the bullpen. But on October 4, the skies had been broomed clean and shone a brilliant blue. Only a few daring white clouds scudded by.

Lavish sunshine bathed grateful Bostonians, their rain gear finally left at home. With summer just two weeks past and a high sun, the afternoon temperature hit a perfect 70 degrees. Visibility was fifteen miles. J. D. Salinger, his fame near its apogee in 1960, had written of "a perfect day for bananafish": a day whose stunning exterior can obscure an underlying threat. As the bright, clear sunny morning broke over eastern Massachusetts, it's not hard to imagine that the mother of one of the marine recruits, whipping up pancakes and eggs for her son's last breakfast at home, looked out the window and exclaimed, "What a great day to fly!"

Like Freddie Abate, most of the other fourteen young Marine recruits had graduated from high school in June, enjoyed summer with hometown buddies after deciding to join the Marine Corps, and—if they were lucky, like Freddie—were leaving behind girlfriends who would write to them at boot camp. In 1960 only 20 percent of Americans had ever flown, so for most of the young marines, this would be their first time on an airplane. In fact, it would be a day of firsts. The novelist Graham Greene wrote, "There comes a time in childhood when a door opens and lets the future in." For the fifteen recruits this was such a time: their first day as proud new marines, first airplane flight, first trip to the South, first trip away from home and family, and facing the thrill and trepidation of boarding a Marine Corps bus at Greenville, South Carolina, to be taken to Parris Island to learn the true meaning of "Semper Fi."

As it turned out, however, the door that opened was to the Lockheed Electra.

With sunset due at 6:21 p.m. and with a breeze now blowing in off the North Atlantic, Mrs. Abate felt a chill on the exposed observation deck. Logan is a peninsular airport, its chin bravely jutting seaward against all comers. The airfield was built on mud flats, as were many coastal city airports of that day: there were no trees to interfere with takeoffs or landings, nothing between pilot and sky except occasional startled birds.

It was unusual that the observation deck would have been almost empty on a sunny afternoon in 1960. Americans of the day were enthralled with aviation, looking to the skies and to the future. Aviation was drawing the best and brightest talent the nation had to offer. A New Englander, Alan Shepard, had recently been named one of the nation's first seven astronauts. Ultimately, he would spend more time on the surface of the moon than anyone else so far: thirty-three and a half hours.

The observation deck at Logan was usually a crowded, giggly place —especially on Sundays, when families brought their children to the airport to watch planes take off and land, and maybe to see a jet or hear it break the sound barrier. But on October 4—while the setting sun seemed to grow in size as it changed color from gold to rose and crimson—there was only one party on the deck: six people with one purpose, to send Freddie off to boot camp with love and laughter. Despite a growing fall chill in the air, the spirits in Freddie's party ran high. The six people gathered close to the railing; smiling and joking, they were looking down at a 45-degree angle at Freddie's plane as it boarded. They had a good view of the aircraft: the entire left side of the plane faced them, and through the windshield they could see the pilot and copilot looking relaxed, sipping coffee as they ran through their preflight checklist.

The Lockheed Electra and its crew had arrived two hours earlier from New York as Eastern Airlines Flight 444. After a scheduled rest stop for the crew, it would be reborn as Eastern 375, with Boston as the starting point for a series of short trips, leapfrogging down the East Coast. Eastern 375 would begin in the gloaming and travel on into the night sky.

A marvel of ease and efficiency, the Lockheed Electra L-188 had joined the U.S. commercial aviation fleet two years before, its arrival much heralded: people in the aviation industry called it a miracle, an exemplar of what Willis Hawkins, president of Lockheed, wrote of airliner design at mid-century: "Airlines were stretching their dreams, the FAA faced with a new invention to approve every day." An airliner's thoughtful new design in action was what the Abate party now observed as the Electra rolled up its sleeves and got ready for work. The plane's functions had been consolidated to speed turnaround at intermediate stops—to improve "on ground performance," in aviation jargon. The left side of the aircraft was devoted to passenger boarding and deplaning, and the right side to refueling, cargo loading, toilet draining, and water replenishing.

At Logan the plane had been topped up with 24,900 pounds of fuel, and the crew calculated the Electra's fully loaded takeoff weight to be 97,987 pounds—evenly distributed and well below maximum. As the Abate party looked on, two attractive young stewardesses— Joan Berry, twenty-two, from Prentice, Mississippi, and Patricia Davies, twenty-three, from Jacksonville, Florida—stood by the Electra's door greeting the marines and the other passengers with their soft, reassuring Southern accents. Joan and Patricia waited for the last two passengers to make their way from asphalt to aircraft on the Electra's new integrated staircase, one of many aeronautical design advances built into the plane. The staircase could be lowered and raised hydraulically from the Electra, with no need for ground crew to roll a staircase out to the aircraft and to fit the two pieces together. In the Electra's design phase, which took place in California—a future-conscious state, especially in the 1950s—self-containment was a watchword for the aeronautical engineers who created the Lockheed L-188.

As the stewardesses watched, an elderly woman made her way up the staircase, followed by Freddie Abate. Freddie was the final passenger to board Eastern 375. After he stepped inside, the staircase was deftly retracted, and the stewardesses shut the Electra's door and locked it fast. Outside the closed door, to the right and low on the fuselage in elegant font was Eastern's new slogan for all Electra flights: "The Golden Falcon Service." The falcon, of course, is a magnificent hunter and among the fastest of avian fliers; some falcons, like the peregrine, plummet from lofty heights at 200 miles per hour to strike small birds in midair—and among their prey is the common starling.

With four mysterious Electra crashes in nineteen months, and Congress in an uproar over the safety of the new airliner, Eastern ticket agents had taken to referring to the aircraft by the handy phrase "our Golden Falcon service." Braniff ticket agents chose to say "our L-188s"; other airlines simply mentioned "our prop-jet service." Air travelers focus their attention on schedule and travel time; they seldom pay attention to type of aircraft. But regular air travelers—the travelers that Eastern Airlines most cared about—had grown jittery about flying the Electra, some business firms quietly telling their traveling staff to avoid the aircraft entirely.

The press corps assigned to cover Lyndon Johnson, the Democrats' vice presidential candidate, had been growing nervous about daily travel on his campaign plane, an Electra, doubtless prompted by calls from their loved ones about the Electra's safety record. The first Electra crash had occurred on February 3, 1959; I will discuss it in chapter 4. In two subsequent, spectacular Electra crashes, six months apart, a wing had torn away from the aircraft in midair. In the first of these, on September 29, 1959, a Braniff Electra crashed into a farmer's field in Buffalo, Texas, with hounds for miles around eerily howling moments before the plane split apart and fell in fiery pieces from the starry skies. The second crash came on March 17, 1960: a 105,000-pound Northwest Electra slammed into a soybean field near Tell City, Indiana, at 618 miles per hour, vanishing in a twelve-foot-deep crater, with the fuselage telescoped to a third of its original length. A total of ninety-seven people died in those two crashes. And a few weeks before the Boston crash, on September 14, 1960, an American Airlines Electra from Boston, this one bound for LaGuardia Airport in New York, had flipped over on landing and hurtled onto the Grand Central Parkway in Queens, where the plane came to a stop upside down. Miraculously, all seventy-six people aboard the full flight survived.

A few moments after Freddie boarded Eastern 375, Mrs. Abate was thrilled to see that her son had settled into a window seat over the left wing, three windows from the door. She could see him plainly and wave to him. In fact he was visible to virtually everyone in the party on the observation deck, seated as he was below the "R" of "PROP" in the legend painted across the fuselage: "FLY EASTERN'S PROP-JET ELECTRA." His friend Harris Wood sat nearby. Pat and Jack joked how "crummy" the plane looked, not realizing that it was relatively new to air transport service, with Lockheed having completed manufacture of the aircraft only sixteen months earlier. The first delivery of an Electra Model L-188 had been to Lockheed's top Electra customer: Eastern Airlines. The Electra did not even take its first flight for Eastern with passengers on board until January 1960. While the aircraft was in development, Eastern had bought a whopping forty Electras at

2.5 million dollars each, with an option to buy thirty more. At the urging of several airlines, the Electra had been designed by Lockheed to nestle perfectly into a lucrative niche in U.S. commercial air travel at that marketing moment—between the reliable but slow piston-engine propeller airliners of yesteryear and the fast pure-jet, or turbojet, airliners that were poised to seize control of long-distance air travel.

Working independently, the Germans and the British had invented the first jet aircraft in 1939 and 1941, respectively. Ever since, braided patterns of global travel by jet-driven commercial airliners had been a heart-thumping dream of the aviation industry and most certainly of long-distance air travelers—who longed for a smooth ride above the weather, at high speed and across vast distances. But, tragically, it had been a dream deferred: the first pure-jet airliner, the four-engine de Havilland Comet, introduced in 1952 by the British, suffered a series of high-profile, catastrophic midair explosions over Europe. The Comet was grounded in 1954, and although its design problems were fixed and the plane put back in the air, the aircraft never regained public trust.

By studying the de Havilland Comet disasters, aeronautical engineers learned that high-flying jetliners required especially sturdy frames to withstand the high pressurization at great altitudes without potentially exploding midflight. By the late 1950s two U.S. jet airliners, the Boeing 707 and the DC-8, had been introduced; unmarked by tragedy, they were ready to seize control of long-distance commercial jet air travel, potentially worldwide. Propeller-driven long-distance airliners, even of the luxury variety, were about to be cast into the dustbin. In 1958 the first of these new airships, the four-engine Boeing 707, was delivered to Pan Am, an airline all about long-distance travel. Yet jetliners could not go everywhere: many of the hundred U.S. airports did not have runways long enough to handle jetliners. Also, pure-jets were not fuel-efficient, although they did better with longer distances than with shorter ones. This was not a big problem, however, for long-distance travel, since passengers were willing to pay more for a speedier arrival and smoother ride. By all accounts pure-jet airliners seemed destined for a golden future, although only in the long-distance market—or so it seemed in the late 1950s. Willy-nilly, the aviation industry as a whole seemed poised to ride an asymptote upward into a boundless future. Indeed, from 1949 until 1980, the number of air travelers in the United States rose dramatically, from 16.7 million to 297 million. Air travel was becoming a vital part of America's business and social fabric.

To occupy the short- and medium-haul air travel niche, a huge profit center in the populous and business-minded United States, an airliner was needed that could travel significantly faster than piston-engine aircraft and that could easily fly in and out of the small-city airports with their short runways. Also, it should be an aircraft that, if necessary, could be tucked into small hangars at small airports. This time the airlines themselves had a specific idea in mind; they were not waiting for an aircraft manufacturer to design something and pitch it to them. They would ask for what they wanted: a hybrid, a turboprop airliner with four propellers rigged to jet engines that could give the plane speed aloft, cutting travel time.

The British Viscount, a turboprop, almost fit the bill, and it had been making inroads into the U.S. market. But the airlines dreamed of a turboprop that fit their business as perfectly as two congruent triangles stacked one atop the other. That meant their full wish list had to be incorporated into one aircraft design; and while they were at it, they hoped a designer could also meet the wish list of the skilled commercial pilots who would fly the new plane. Many of the commercial pilots of that era were no-nonsense former combat pilots, well tested in World War II and in Korea. The pilots wanted a responsive aircraft, alive with reserve power, forgiving of small errors, and engineered for a workaday job.

If the Lockheed Electra L-188 looked "crummy" to Pat and Jack, Freddie Abate's girlfriend and friend, it was because of its functional design. No aviation poets would write of its sleek lines or swept-back wings, compare it to the regal condor or eagle, or compose an ode to its Grecian beauty or classic proportions. The Electra was elegant only in the sense that its design was utilitarian, jammed full of brand-new, user-friendly engineering features: the plane ready to take control of the market it was designed for and to push to one side the old, piston-driven propeller aircraft, notorious for drone, vibration, and over-heated, cramped cabins.

As Pat would report later, "I don't know what I was expecting." For sure, she hadn't expected the Electra, which had something of an odd-duck look, with its stubby wings and 13-foot long, squarish propellers. The airlines had invited the great U.S. aircraft manufacturers to bid on a design for a new turboprop-jet airliner, one that could get up and down fast, was fuel efficient, flew at least 100 miles per hour faster than piston-engine planes, offered cabin comfort to passengers, and was a splendid flying machine for pilots. Lockheed won the contract. For the first time ever, airlines and commercial pilots had ongoing input into an airliner's design, from start to finish. The resulting Electra L-188 could fly nearly 450 miles per hour, turn around in twelve minutes at intermediate stops and be quickly back in the air where it liked to be, like a great pet dog off for a romp. It was an airplane ideal for a series of destinations 150 to 800 miles apart; one with high lift and forward power that could get in and out of airports with short runways. But, if desired, the Electra could handle distances of up to 2,200 miles, allowing it to service long-distance, low-traffic runs that might be bypassed by pure-jets as unprofitable. The Electra's wings were short enough so the aircraft could be tucked into small hangars; but to compensate for their shortness, the wings were broad enough to produce huge lift and forward power.

The Electra had four highly reliable General Motors Allison jet turbine engines, which had been battle tested on the military's C-130 transports. The Electra had plenty of reserve power, never dawdled, did its job, and rose from short runways like a hawk. No wonder Eastern Airlines loved the plane, as did the pilots who flew it. Eastern would flood the East Coast corridor, with Electras sewing up the moneymaking short- and medium-hop routes. At the approval stage, the Electra L-188 had inspired confidence: it was the most pretested airliner in aviation history, on the ground and in the air, and it had gained certification from federal aviation authorities five weeks early, far exceeding requirements in a number of categories.

With its wide spacious cabin, the Electra was passenger friendly—its seats ample and comfortable, and its Sky Lounge matching the lounges of luxury-class airliners, offering diffused lighting, wide seats, and, on some of the planes, the finishing touch of tabletop lamps.

The most modern designs for passenger and crew comfort handled heating, air conditioning, and cabin pressure and delivered a quiet ride. Lockheed had outfitted Eastern's Electras with sixty-five cabin seats, six seats in the lounge, and provisions for five crew members: seventy-six souls could fly comfortably.

Despite the Electra's string of four crashes in nineteen months, commercial pilots, always conservative, bid heavily to fly the plane, with pilots of high seniority and experience usually winning out.

The Electra that Freddie Abate boarded on October 4, 1960, perfectly matched this profile of Eastern Airlines's intended business use of the Electra and of a crew marked by strong experience.

Eastern 375 was scheduled to fly in the late afternoon to Philadelphia, where it would leave its returning conventioneers and its baseball fans, who would surely chatter during the flight about the Yankees' pitcher, Art Ditmar, and what a great a high-school ballplayer he had been on Boston's North Shore. Some passengers may have known him personally, as he was born in Winthrop and now lived in adjacent Revere, Massachusetts. This season Ditmar had outperformed even his legendary teammate, Yankee pitching ace Whitey Ford. In Philadelphia the baseball fans would switch flights for Pittsburgh. Eastern 375 would continue to Charlotte and then Greenville, where it would drop off the marine recruits, and fly on to Atlanta, its last stop. With nearly all seats filled, this flight would make money for Eastern.

Had the passengers and their families reviewed the credentials of the crew on the flight deck, they would have been impressed. The pilot, Captain Curtis W. Fitts, fifty-nine, of Bell Meadow, Georgia, was a twenty-six-year veteran with Eastern. He had 23,000 hours of flying time, with almost 1,100 hours in the left seat—the pilot's seat—of the Electra. Since the aircraft had been introduced less than two years earlier, few pilots probably had more experience flying the Electra than Captain Fitts. Copilot Martin J. Calloway of Atlanta was just one day short of seven years with Eastern. The flight engineer, Malcolm Hall of Memphis, Tennessee, had been with the airline a full seven years. Hall held airframe and power plant—or engine—certificates, which meant he understood the aircraft's structure and how the Allison turboprop engines operated inside and out. The flight engineer's job was to monitor and control all aircraft systems during takeoff and cruise, relieving the pilots to fly the aircraft and make timely decisions. Hall's tasks included keeping tabs on and adjusting engine power of the four turboprops as needed on takeoff and in flight. Both pilots had passed the Federal Aviation Administration's stringent Class I health examinations, required of those who fly commercial aircraft; the flight engineer, had passed the Class II health examination, required for his post. Flight deck crews are given periodic "line checks" to confirm their skills and competencies; Fitts, Calloway, and Hall had all passed line checks in recent months. In short, this crew was fully fit to fly this aircraft on this day.

With stunning weather and a highly experienced crew, all sixty-seven passengers and five crew members on Eastern 375 had every reason to expect a lovely sunset flight over the 271 miles from Boston to Philadelphia. They would cover the distance in under ninety minutes. In 1776, on his way to the Second Continental Congress that would declare American independence, John Adams needed fifteen days to make the same journey on horseback—a journey fraught with far more danger than a flight on a modern Lockheed Electra. Eastern's passengers could lean back, relax, pull out the evening edition of one of Boston's several daily newspapers of that time, and read about the Kennedy-Nixon debates, the strike at General Electric's Aircraft Division in Lynn, or World Series news.

At about 5:30 p.m., the flight crew of Eastern 375 fired up the Electra's engines. Pat and Jack found it "funny" that the two right engines started right away, but not the left two, which started and then stopped. "My eyes were on the propellers," Pat later said. "They didn't start like the other two did. I believe it was the number two that started first. . . . It went around a couple of times and then stopped. Then number one turned around and then stopped—I don't think it stopped [again] after it [finally] started. After this, number two started again." The left-side engines were turning slowly at first. But once the engines were operating normally, the pilot spent no additional time warming them up.

At 5:33, Captain Fitts initiated his first contact with Logan's tower: "Eastern 375. IFR to Philadelphia." "IFR" stands for instrument flight rules and means the pilot is qualified to fly solely based on instrument data and plans to do so—for instance, when nothing is visible out the pilot's windshield but clouds.

Obviously mistaking Eastern 375's call letters, the tower controller replied: "Eastern 435 cleared to Runway 9. Wind is southeast one zero." The controller passed on other data in aviation parlance to Captain Fitts, cleared a TWA plane onto Runway 9, and, in accordance with procedure, turned the TWA plane and Eastern 375 over to the jurisdiction of the "clearance delivery" controller for additional instructions.

At 5:35, with the controller's clearing him to taxi to Runway 9, his takeoff runway, Captain Fitts began to roll his aircraft and simultaneously to arc it to the right, toward Runway 9. At that point Freddie Abate's brother-in-law memorized the airplane's U.S. Registry number, N-5533, painted on the tail, to help the family identify it once on the runway. At exactly that moment, 5:35 p.m., the water in Boston Harbor hit low tide. The mud flats all around Logan now were fully exposed, providing delightful seaside and sunset dining to the airport's well-known bird life. Having poured out gold all day, the sun continued its downward plunge. The ambient light began shifting toward rose as the crimson sun sank behind the Boston skyline.

The thousands of starlings along the end of Runway 9 had finished their dining and given themselves a cleaning dip in seawater, and were preparing to head straight for their night-time roost—probably under the sheltering superstructure of the Mystic River Bridge.

The TWA flight on Runway 9 was cleared and took off. Captain Fitts checked in again, and the clearance delivery controller gave him the following instruction, essentially giving back to Fitts the flight plan he had submitted earlier: "Air Traffic Control clears E375 to Philadelphia Airport." Once airborne, Captain Fitts was to hold an easterly takeoff heading for two minutes, ascend to 3,000 feet, and then turn westerly toward the air traffic intersection at Natick, Massachusetts, after which he would fly to Philadelphia, at an altitude of 10,000 feet. With professionalism, Captain Fitts repeated the controller's instruction.

As the plane turned right and peeled carefully and slowly away from the observation deck, Freddie and the boys on board were all waving to the Abate party, and everyone in the party was waving back. Mrs. Abate kept her eyes glued to her son's window over the left wing until the plane had turned fully away and he was no longer visible. But she continued to watch the plane closely, never taking her eyes off it, walking along with it on the observation deck as if paralleling its path. When Eastern 375 reached Runway 9, it halted on the taxiway, awaiting permission to swing left onto the takeoff runway.

On a nearby runway, one restricted to the airport's infrequent pure-jet traffic (and, when the pure-jets weren't using it, often inhabited by bird life), Logan tower cleared two F-86 Sabre Jets that took off in formation, powered by J-47 turbojet engines made nine miles away in Lynn, perhaps touched by my father's own hands. The jets quickly headed skyward. With jet propulsion and sweet aerodynamics, the Sabre Jets could reach an altitude of 8,000 feet in sixty seconds; they could rise up from sea level four times faster than the Electra. In a few seconds the twin jets could be seen circling hundreds of feet above Logan; their white contrails writing America's pure-jet future against the cobalt blue sky.

On board Eastern 375, as it readied to make its left turn onto "Runway niner," passengers and crew were buckled in their seats, as instructed by Joan Berry and Patricia Davies, themselves buckled into seats in the rear of the aircraft in the Sky Lounge, on the left side. Seated directly across from them was Dudley Ward, the forty-year-old treasurer of the Scott Paper Company in Wallingford, Pennsylvania, a former resident of Hingham, Massachusetts, and a Navy pilot in World War II. Ward had boarded the plane fifteen minutes before departure and been reading the evening newspaper, not paying much attention to what was going on. "Everything seemed to be going along about normal," he later reported. As other passengers boarded, a man approached Ward and told him he was sitting in his seat. So Ward moved rearward to a seat in the Sky Lounge, an even more pleasant location to be reading his newspaper, with its living room atmosphere and diffused lighting.

As the Electra was waiting for the tower's okay to turn onto Runway 9 and position itself for takeoff, some 400 feet above Logan Airport, positioned over the East Boston Expressway and awaiting permission to land, was a seven-seat business executive plane, an Aero Commander, inbound from New York. On board were three veteran airmen. The Aero Commander was the only aircraft waiting to land, scheduled to come in on Runway 15, which intersected Runway 9. So the three airmen had their eyes glued on the Electra, waiting for it to clear Runway 9. The Aero Commander happened to be the type of aircraft chosen by President Eisenhower as the first official aircraft of the president of the United States. The Aero Commander's copilot was Sheldon Lewis of Elmira, New York, the editor of *Skyways* magazine. At Lewis's request, the pilot, Jack Riggs, had flown over the moth-balled baby flattop *Salerno Bay*, tied up at the South Boston Annex of the Charlestown Navy Yard. As a marine pilot in the South Pacific in World War II, Lewis had regularly taken off from the *Salerno Bay*.

The chief Logan controller directed a number of other aircraft in and out of the airport. Captain Fitts checked in once again: "Eastern 375 ready for takeoff on 9." The tower replied, "Eastern 375 taxi into position and hold."

The Eastern flight swung left onto Runway 9, the left side of the aircraft once again visible to the Abate party on the observation deck. Mrs. Abate knew where to look for Freddie—over the left wing and under the "R." Freddie's party would have an excellent view of the Electra as it took off, speeding past them from right to left, west to east.

At 5:39 p.m., four minutes after Eastern 375 had begun to taxi toward Runway 9, the tower controller had his final exchange with Captain Fitts, after addressing the Aero Commander.

Tower to the Aero Commander: "53B, start your base-leg now."
53B [pilot Jack Riggs]: "Okay."
Tower to Captain Fitts: "Eastern 375 cleared for immediate takeoff Runway niner."
EA 375 [Captain Fitts]: "375 rolling."

Although he had a microphone attached to his throat, those would be the last words of Curtis W. Fitts. Officials later said, "All he had to do was say 'May Day,' and the control tower would have received his message."

After a ground roll of 2,500 feet, attaining a velocity of 139 miles per hour, the Boston Electra lifted from Runway 9. Jack Riggs, Sheldon Lewis, and John Rathbone, a third skilled pilot sitting in the jump seat of the Aero Commander, had their eyes fixed on the Electra.

From the observation deck, Freddie's mom watched the Electra's takeoff roll and acceleration, and saw the plane's nose rotate up from the surface of Runway 9 as 100,000 pounds of aircraft, fuel, passengers, crew, and baggage became airborne in defiance of any earthling's common sense. She saw the Electra's landing gear retract, which can boost an aircraft's lift by reducing drag by as much as 50 percent. The Electra was striving to attain "the wind-swept heights with easy grace, where never lark nor even eagle flew"—where the nineteen-year-old John Gillespie Magee Jr., once "put out my hand, and touched the face of God," shortly before being killed in a midair collision during World War II. Portions of Magee's poem "High Flight" can be found on the gravestones of many aviators and astronauts at Arlington National Cemetery. President Ronald Reagan quoted from the poem as he eulogized the seven *Challenger* astronauts who were lost on a cold, bright day in January 1986, when the shuttle exploded seventy-three seconds after takeoff.

But the flight of the Electra in Boston didn't even last seventy-three seconds, or surpass 285 feet in altitude, far shy of wind-swept heights. It never flew above heights that larks, eagles, or starlings can easily attain. Just as the landing gear retracted, Freddie's mom saw a ball of fire flash between the two wheels of the aircraft. With a mother's eyes, she was the only one in the Abate party to see it; the protective cloak of a mother's care is never fully withdrawn, even when your son is a member of the U.S. Marine Corps. Here, edited and condensed, is Mrs. Abate's report to the Civil Aeronautics Board, then—in the days before the National Transportation Safety Board—the federal agency charged with finding out the causes of aviation accidents and recommending needed changes:

> I saw a flash. The plane tipped over on its left wing and down it came. It was like someone flashing a big light. When it came down, we saw the splash. Then we saw nothing. I watched the landing gear go up; that's when I saw a ball of fire between the two wheels. The color and size of the flash looked like a headlight. Didn't hear motors, didn't hear anything. It was very, very quiet. It seemed that everything was dead. I could see the plane very well. I never took my eyes off it. It hap-

pened very, very fast. It was going straight and it was rising, kept rising. It seemed as though it was turning a little to take its course. It didn't appear to be very far. It wasn't up very long when it came down.

Freddie's father told the Civil Aeronautics Board: "We saw a splash of water. Then the plane disappeared out of sight. Right then and there I knew there was no hope. It got real quiet, and all of a sudden everything stopped. It had dropped down like a dead weight."

Freddie's mother, father, and everyone else in their party noted that the Electra took off very slowly, a perception probably influenced by the fact that they had just watched the takeoff of two F-86 Sabre Jets. The Sabre Jet not only held the world airspeed record for six consecutive years, it is reportedly the first aircraft to have broken the sound barrier. At takeoff and in its initial climb, the Electra's speed was later determined by the CAB to have been normal for the conditions.

Everyone in the group also noted an uncanny silence. Freddie's sister told the CAB:

> The plane went down on Freddie's side and then it was gone—we didn't see it anymore. I didn't see anything like smoke or vapor. I saw something white and that was the splash.
>
> I heard the engines. Then all of a sudden there was not a sound anywhere. There was noise and the next second no noise—just still. There was no sound even of the crash where we were. When it started to take off, I ran down that way because I was watching the windows; then all of a sudden it tipped and went down.

Jimmy Crawford, Freddie's brother-in-law, was a precise observer:

> I remember Mrs. Abate saying something about the ball of fire. I think it [the plane] was making a left turn, but it seemed too low to make a left turn. It came up at a pretty sharp angle—about 15 degrees. It was gaining altitude across the length of the runway. It seemed as if it was going to make a turn—then it started to go down. I could then see whole top of aircraft; the nose seemed to be 30 degrees below the horizon. I came back later and looked through the telescope. No smoke, fire—saw nothing. It seemed to go down very slowly; that is why I kept

thinking that it was really higher and that it was going to pull out of it. It was not an abrupt stop of engines; it must have been a gradual reduction in sound.

Freddie's pal Jack noted the left wing tipping, first right, then left: "I estimate [the plane was] about 300 feet off the ground. The left wing was sort of [tipped up] toward the right, then it banked left, hit the water, and nothing. I didn't hear anything; the wheels came up and it started to climb—then all of a sudden everything went dead. Mrs. Abate mentioned something about a ball of fire. I didn't see the ball of fire."

And Freddie's girlfriend, Pat, told the CAB: "All I saw was the plane go up, tip, and drop. Mother Abate said the plane had crashed. It was completely gone. We were helpless—there was nothing we could do. I didn't know the splash was water. I thought it was smoke. I didn't see any water. His plane went down, stopped. It seemed as if something just died and fell."

Fifty-two and a half seconds after Eastern 375 began its takeoff roll, Jack Riggs, the pilot of the Aero Commander, barked into his mike: "Tower, an Electra just went into the drink. . . . I saw a flame on number two."

From their perfect aerial view, 400 feet in the sky, the three veteran airmen on the Aero Commander had watched helplessly—horror-struck, hearts in their throats—the death throes of an airliner with seventy-two souls on board. The flight of the Electra from "375 rolling" to its crash into the bay had lasted only forty-seven and a half seconds. In 1960, Otis Davis, who set a world record in the 400-meter dash at the summer Olympic Games in Rome, would have run his race and been recuperating for just over two and a half seconds in the time it took for Eastern 375 to begin and end its life.

Myron Williams, a freelance photographer who had gained permission from Logan officials to be near Runway 9, snapped two photos of the Electra one second apart before its plunge into Winthrop Bay. Like Abraham Zapruder in Dallas in 1963, Williams was not intending anything other than a playful use of his camera. Both of Williams's photographs caught the Electra at 121 feet in the air. In the first photo, the nose was up slightly, and the plane was banking slightly to the left. But, in the second, the nose was up more, and the plane was banking sharply leftward.

The more the aircraft turned left and banked left, the more the left wing was shielded from the vital airflow that creates lift, the force that keeps a plane aloft. The plane itself was now blocking airflow to its own left wing. The left wing was about to stall—or have insufficient lift to keep aloft, causing the wing to fall by force of gravity and sending the aircraft spiraling downward on the near vertical.

By the time of Williams's photo sequence, the plane had gone into what pilots call a mush: it had become an aircraft that could no longer be controlled. The Electra had lost more than half its altitude, down to 121 feet from its maximum of 285 feet, and was sinking fast. Gravity was reaching up and grabbing at the aircraft, pulling it downward. The men in the cockpit surely knew the worst: they were going into the water, they had no fighting chance; the crew had become passengers.

By now the Electra had cleared the end of Runway 9 and was at the edge of the sea. In airport nomenclature, Runway 9 means pointed toward a compass heading of 90 degrees: due east. But, as the Electra left sea-girt Logan airfield, it was way off course: it had veered sharply left, toward the north and away from its assigned due east heading. Instead, it was on a new heading of 30 degrees, north by northeast—not toward Magee's wind-swept heights, but toward Winthrop's Cottage Park Yacht Club and the beckoning Winthrop Bay.

As the Electra had cleared the end of the airfield, Bartholomew Flynn, a corrections officer at Deer Island Prison, a mile and a half to the southeast, was watching his dog from the window of his living quarters in the Old Master's House. When he had gotten home from work he had given some medicine to his dog, who had been sick for several days, and tied him up twenty feet below on the lawn. As he watched his dog, Flynn was facing toward Logan and Winthrop Harbor. Resting on the seawater slightly beyond the end of Runway 9 was a group of cormorants, which Flynn identified by their elongated necks and intense black color. He saw the aircraft pass over the edge of the airport and out over the water, taking note that the Electra was flying too low, swaying from side to side, wings dipping now left, now right.

"She came down low over the water, and the group of birds resting on the water flew up against her," Flynn said, commenting that the majority of the cormorants hit the body of the plane. To him, it looked as though the pilot had "pulled her nose up at a very sharp angle, much sharper than other operators of large planes do, but not as sharp as the military planes." And "there appeared to be two trails of smoke from her engines, one from each side of her body." Flynn told the CAB: "I glanced back at the airport and saw three large groups of starlings flying above where the plane left. There were hundreds in each group, flying as if violently disturbed. The plane was now over the Winthrop side of the bay—floating in the air, as if about to drop down and land."

Flynn watched the aircraft struggle, tipping left and right repeatedly. He saw it do a half-barrel roll to the left, turn on its back, and appear to be in an arch for some seconds. Flynn thought it might break in two. Then it seemed to back down on its tail, and he thought it might actually fall from the sky tail first. But suddenly "she jumps forward and falls on her engines . . . almost perpendicular when she hits the water. A great cloud of spray comes up and one of her wings turns over in the spray."

From Flynn's vantage point, the Electra appeared to be flying at an altitude equal to the rooftops of houses along the Winthrop shore: "I think she would have hit or scraped their roofs at the level she was at when the cormorants smashed into her." He saw no flashes or fire, only two lines of smoke trailing from engines.

"She appeared to be sound when she hit the water," Flynn said in what surely seems an odd eulogy to Eastern Airlines Flight 375. But later it would be found that three of the four turboprop engines were working at the instant the aircraft struck the water. In Flynn's report to the CAB, he added as a sad valediction: "I hope you find something in this report that will help avert future crashes. I wished to God I never saw this one, as it left me with a bad case of hypertension."

Sheldon Lewis, the copilot of the Aero Commander, told *The Boston Globe* that the airmen in his plane above the Electra had watched it make a very steep bank and a steep climb to the left—a highly unusual maneuver for a plane the size of the Electra. They had then watched the plane do "a wingover"—turning over on its back—and plunge into the bay: "His nose was straight down. He was over the water and hit it on the vertical." They watched the tail break off: "The tail never got wet before it hit the water. It must have been the impact of the nose hitting the bottom that broke it off."

Indeed. Robert Jenkins, twenty-two, of Dorchester, who was later in the bay wearing scuba gear, discovered two very deep furrows running twenty or thirty yards along the mossy bottom, showing the aircraft's momentum after impact with terra firma thirty feet under water. Lewis recollected the Aero Commander's call to the Logan tower to tell them that the plane had crashed into the bay: "There was what seemed like an awful silence on communication. Then came the reply: 'Yes, we saw it, and we have alerted crash equipment.'"

"From the whole thing it would appear to me the pilot lost full power on one engine and partial power on another to make him roll the way he did," Lewis observed. "No pilot worth his salt would let that happen to him unless these factors happened."

"Our reaction was one of horror—sheer stark horror," he added. "All of us have seen planes crash before, but never this close up." The men on the Aero Commander considered landing and taxiing to the water's edge to help, but they saw that the plane had crashed too far out into the bay for them to be of help. The best thing to do, they decided, was to land and get out of the way. A. S. Plotkin of the *Globe* wrote of the three airmen: "None had ever witnessed an air tragedy on so big a scale this close up before." "I hope I never see it again," Lewis said.

Jeanne Vitigliano, age seventeen, and her mother had heard a noise while in their Winthrop shore home, "not thinking too much of it. . . . The jets here make so much noise." But when she looked outside, she saw the whole length of a plane in the water, with the front section missing: "I saw three or four persons swimming near it. . . . By the time we got our coats on, it had disappeared." The front section sank quickly, but the long rear section floated for some minutes before sinking.

The Masone family had sat down to supper in their Woodside Park home, across Winthrop Bay from Logan Airport, at 5:30 p.m. Ten minutes later they heard "a screeching sound and a loud explosion . . . nothing I'd ever heard before," Evelyn Masone told the *Globe*.

But it was her ten-year-old niece, Michelle Berg, who said, "Maybe a plane crashed." Mrs. Masone ran to her back porch, overlooking the water, and shouted, "My God, a plane is sinking." She later reported: "It was sinking as I watched . . . in two parts."

Several Winthrop observers told the *Globe* that the aircraft banked sharply left, with one wing hitting the water first, and then the Electra's nose striking the bay with such force that the plane "seemed to fly apart." Lieutenant Commander Everett Cook, U.S. Navy Reserve, watched as the plane hit the water among small pleasure craft anchored off the yacht club: "It appeared to split wide open . . . within minutes the rest of the plane had disappeared." One witness, a state aeronautics inspector, reported: "The plane rose . . . then suddenly dropped half the distance to the water." The aircraft banked to the left, "as though the pilot was trying to gain altitude and get back to the airport, and then it went down." Scores of residents reported they thought a jet had broken the sound barrier.

The home of Peter French, Winthrop's town counsel, overlooked the crash site. He was sitting at his dining room table when he "heard a loud thump like a jet plane breaking the sound barrier. . . . I looked out of the window and saw the plane falling into the water. There was a loud explosion. The tail seemed to come off. The wing seemed to separate and parts of it flew up into the air. . . . A big shower of white dust or spray came up. I ran to the phone and called the police."

When the plane struck the bay, it struck nose first, but with a marked tilt toward its left wing—Freddie Abate's wing. The nose and left wing took the full impact of a 100,000-pound aircraft striking the ocean in a free fall from 121 feet into thirty feet of water. A geyser of white spray shot skyward. The left wing shattered into bits, its broken pieces later washing up onto the Winthrop shore. Ten minutes before the crash, the Abate party had watched Freddie smiling and waving goodbye to those he loved most in the world from his comfortable Electra seat overlooking the left wing. The Boston morning papers on Monday, October 5, would report that Frederick Nino Abate, age eighteen, had been killed in a plane crash in Boston Harbor. He was among the first fatalities ever at Logan Airport, and one of twelve Marine Corps recruits who died one minute after takeoff.

3 Fading October Light

And in the harbor a geyser of spray settled as rapidly as it rose.
The body of a giant airliner, ripped asunder by impact, and now
wingless, settled slowly. —Ed McGrath, *The Boston Globe*

This was not a crash that you would expect anybody to survive.
It was not what is called a survivable crash.
—Alan Boyd, chairman, Civil Aeronautics Board

When the 100,000-pound Electra fell out of the October
sky from 121 feet up, it struck the bay with incredible kinetic energy.
Using rough calculations from kinematics (that branch of mechanics
concerned with the motion of objects without reference to the forces
that cause the motion), the aircraft had 178 megajoules of energy at
its point of impact with the water. "Simply put, that's a lot," said Adam
Libert, the brilliant University of Pennsylvania engineering sciences
student who did the computations. The Electra's energy on impact
was roughly equivalent to an AK-47 firing 90,000 bullets at the same
time, or 200 average-sized sedans driving simultaneously into a wall
at eighty miles per hour. No surprise, then, that Alan Boyd, the Civil
Aeronautics Board's chairman, stated, after the official investigation,
that the crash of the Boston Electra "was not what is called a survivable crash." But ten of the seventy-two people on board did survive,
and still others were rescued and given at least a fighting chance to
survive, even though they died later.

How was this possible in a nonsurvivable crash? Some of it was
luck—where the passengers were seated on the aircraft. When Dudley

Ward was asked to move and shifted to a seat in the sky lounge, deep in the tail section, he boosted his chances of survival, given the nature of the crash—with the aircraft's nose and left wing tip striking first, absorbing the full impact of 300 g's of deceleration. Some of the g's were dissipated when the aircraft split apart, as the tail broke off and hit the water still dry, with its structure comparatively intact. While Ward survived the crash, along with the stewardesses, Joan Berry and Patricia Davies, who were sitting across from him, they had still crashed in thirty feet of water, more than deep enough to drown in.

Everyone on board who survived the crash was in a shocked state. Some were in medical shock. Most were gravely injured, not able to save themselves. They were in water-laden street clothes and cast into deep water, while strapped into an airliner seat that had torn loose from the floor of the plane—as happened to all seats but two. Without speedy rescue, nearly all alive would die.

The survival of ten people is the result of the swift, sure action of citizen responders from the Winthrop shore and of a massive rescue and recovery mobilization unmatched in Boston annals. One newspaper headline the next day would read, using Boston's nickname of "The Hub": "Hub's Biggest Rescue Mobilization."

Rescue and Recovery: A Précis
> Out in the harbor breaths of smoke
> are rising from the water, sea-smoke
> some call it or breath of souls
> —Olga Broumas, "Mercy"

The first rescuers to reach the downed Electra were owners of pleasure craft from the Winthrop shore; dinghies and skiffs pressed into action—boys and men often not stopping for oars as they took to the water, but snatching up planks as makeshift paddles. Other Winthrop residents slogged through knee-deep, oil-smeared mud, trying to reach victims carried their way by currents and the new inbound tide. Deep mud proved an ongoing hazard as rescuers struggled to carry the living and dead to dry land; soon unending relays of stretcher bearers slipped and stumbled across the tidal flats.

"Young boys suddenly took on the stature of men. They saw death for the first time and they were heroic," wrote Ed McGrath, a reporter for *The Boston Globe*, as he described the hellish scene:

> Victims floated by in macabre tableau, still strapped to their seats, erect, silent, dead. Crimson sunset and the red of blood streaked the darkening harbor waters. Those who lived neither shrieked nor moaned. They clung in stunned shock to mooring lines of small boats, to debris and to their drifting seats. Boys and men paddled by bobbing dead to reach the living; the waters reeked of fuel oil and gasoline.

Seats continually popped to the surface, bodies strapped in them, punctuating rescue efforts. One dead woman floated past rescue workers still clutching her purse. Rev. John Burns, an East Boston priest, waded into the bay to give last rites to thirty floating bodies.

Hundreds of police, firefighters, and civil defense officers from as far away as Worcester descended on the scene, as well as Coast Guard helicopters and boats, navy ships, medical personnel, and clergy. One hundred and fifty police and civilian skin divers slipped from small craft into the inky, freezing water. Divers were ferried by basket from Runway 9 to the dive site by Coast Guard helicopters that returned with the injured. Fourteen- and fifteen-year-old boys triaged from small boats—giving a thumb up or down to chopper pilots ferrying the living and gravely injured to waiting rescue vehicles. Ambulances lined up fifty deep on the Winthrop shore. Women poured out from Winthrop homes, carrying blankets for the victims, or tugging garden carts or pushing wheelbarrows piled high with donuts and gallons of coffee for the growing brigade of rescue workers. Here again is Ed McGrath:

> The sounds of disaster became the sounds of rescue—the plopping frogmen as they struggled through the mud flats that swallowed their feet . . . the sirens, rising in crescendo from every direction . . . the whispered prayers of priests over bodies of the dead and dying . . . the growl of helicopters skimming the bay . . . the impatient orders of rescue teams, trying to bring order to the chaos of arriving and departing apparatus, of descending crowds and armadas of small boats.

The spontaneous heroism and generosity of that day was not without a countercurrent: mindless sightseers clogged Winthrop streets already crowded by the evening rush hour, blocking rescue vehicles; the East Boston Tunnel finally shut down to all but rescue traffic.

Furiously, rescuers worked against the fading October light: they sought the living but mostly found the dead. As night started to fall, the tide began to carry the bodies and debris toward the East Boston shore. Two hundred searchers—public safety officers and volunteers—formed a three-mile human chain from Winthrop to East Boston and waded, fully dressed, up to their shoulders into the chilly waters. Divers worked through the night in murky to pitch-black water to bring up the dead; as darkness descended, the scene was luridly lit by floodlights and the carbon arc lamps of low-circling Coast Guard helicopters.

One sixteen-year-old, John J. Goglia, already a pilot and trained scuba diver, felt his East Boston home shake with the crash. Within an hour, John was under the water, the visibility so poor he had to search for victims by hand, recovering only body parts and bringing them to the surface. Decades later, President Bill Clinton would appoint Goglia to two five-year terms on the National Transportation Safety Board; he is the only member so far to hold an aircraft mechanic's certificate. Goglia grew up so near Logan that he never used an alarm clock: at 7:00 a.m. every day, he'd awaken as mechanics started up airplane engines. Circling Logan on his three-speed Raleigh bicycle, Goglia fell in love with planes. He became an aircraft mechanic and ultimately one of the nation's top crash experts—a defender of the public good and a man of unsleeping integrity, fighting passionately for safer planes, safer transportation in general, and more compassionate treatment of victims' families. The media dubbed John Goglia "the patron saint of travel safety," and he himself said—in an article in the spring 2005 issue of *Magis*, a magazine published by Saint Louis University's Parks College of Engineering, Aviation, and Technology— "I've probably cried more on national TV than anybody else." His life's compass heading was set October 4, 1960, when radiating megajoules of energy rocked his East Boston home.

Dress Blues
Sixty-two people died in the crash of Eastern 375, more than in all prior New England commercial crashes combined. With so many

deaths, it seems odd somehow that 90 percent of the U.S. mail on the plane was recovered, dried out, and went on to lead a normal life. Federal agents in boats surrounding the salvage scene took custody of the secret missile-system plans brought on board the Electra in a sealed briefcase, but the engineer who had carried those plans was dead.

In a noble and touching moment, the assistant commandant of the U.S. Marine Corps said of the twelve marines who had been killed: "They were just as much marines as I am"—even though they had been marines for only a few hours. Their parents were told that their sons could be buried in dress blue uniforms. The first to be buried, Harvey Gorewitz, eighteen, of Dorchester, a graduate of Boston Technical High School, was laid to rest in dress blues, while an honor guard of ten marines fired a volley in tribute. Rabbi Myer Strassfeld of Congregation Agudath Israel officiated at the funeral, before a cortege of thirty-five cars wended its sorrowful way to the Jewish cemetery in West Roxbury, where Kaddish was said at the graveside.

Voices from the Bay: "I Have to Get to Greenland"
Right after Evelyn Masone cried out from her rear porch, "My God, a plane is sinking!" her eighteen-year-old son, Jim, shouted, "Come on, Dad! Let's go!" In those five words is the elegant, well-machined key that unlocks the puzzle of how ten people survived a nonsurvivable crash.

Jim and his dad, James, forty-eight, raced to the Cottage Park Yacht Club. Evelyn took her daughters, thirteen-year-old Jean and eight-year-old Sharon, and her niece Michelle, ten, and ran out into the street. A quiet suburban neighborhood was suddenly flooded with people all of one mind: everyone was rushing to the water's edge. Jim and his dad were joined at the yacht club by their neighbors William Kirby; James Evans, and his sons James Jr. and Kenneth; and James Reed. They yanked rowboats off the pier and passed out oars from a locker. But none of the rowboats had oarlocks.

On September 12, Hurricane Donna had slammed into southeast Connecticut with winds gusting up to 130 miles per hour; the storm had then slashed diagonally through Massachusetts into Maine, not dissipating until it reached Quebec. Donna produced pockets of four to eight inches of rain and drove a storm surge five to ten feet high. It was the only storm on record to deliver hurricane-force winds in Florida, the mid-Atlantic states, and New England. The hurricane killed 364 and caused over $500 million in damage. So bad was Donna its name was retired from further hurricane service. Anticipating the storm's fury, some Winthrop residents had pulled their small boats from the water early that season, often removing oarlocks. That did not stop the Masones and other civilian rescuers, who put the boats into the water and paddled, not rowed, typically with only one oar, to the crash site 200 yards offshore. The main section of the Electra had barely sunk before Winthrop residents were on the blue waters of the harbor, paddling furiously toward the crash scene.

The Masones in their rowboat spotted an African American man floating face up, the first passenger to be rescued. As unlikely as it seems, he was clutching a Bible in one hand. As the Masones approached, the man was yelling, "Help me! Help me!" and "Don't leave my friend." Below him in the water, the Masones saw two passengers grimly floating face down in the bay. With his free hand, the man desperately held onto the body of his friend. The Masones struggled to pull the living victim on board but soon realized that they first had to unstrap him from his passenger seat. Keeping a rowboat from capsizing while pulling a grown man aboard, especially with the added weight of water-soaked street clothes, is difficult—and made even more difficult without two oars fixed in oarlocks to steady the craft. Jim loosened the man's belt and tried again, but the man was covered in oil and kept slipping from Jim's grasp. The Masones finally got him on board and paddled back toward the gathering crowd on the Winthrop shore.

When the Electra struck the bay and flew apart like a child's toy, much of its nearly 25,000 pounds of jet fuel was set free. Since oil is lighter than water, it floated to the top of the seawater and was rapidly coating Winthrop Harbor with highly flammable Jet A fuel. When Ed McGrath of the *Globe* filed his initial news story, he wrote: "The pungent smell of gasoline marked the disaster site like an invisible buoy." As hundreds of rescuers descended upon Winthrop Harbor, Jet A fuel was creating the danger of a lake of fire," to use a phrase from the book of Revelations—also known as the book of the Apocalypse: "And death and hell were cast into the lake of fire."

Jet A fuel is a mix of kerosene and gasoline, with a flashpoint of 100 degrees Fahrenheit. Flashpoint is the temperature at which the vapor hovering above a flammable liquid will ignite in air, usually lower than the temperature needed to ignite the liquid itself.

Any one of the hundreds of rescuers at the scene could have a tossed a lit cigarette, dropped a lit flare, or been driving a powerboat with an overheated engine. Recall that it was the age of smokers. If so, the harbor could have erupted in fast-flowing, billowing golden and red flames. If the concept of a water fire seems an oxymoron, remember the Cuyahoga River fire in 1969 in northeast Ohio, when oil and floating debris ignited. And not for the first time: the Cuyahoga had caught fire in 1868, 1912, 1936, 1952, and 1969, earning it the sobriquet "the river that oozes rather than flows." The 1969 fire did have one positive outcome: along with Rachel Carson's *Silent Spring*, it led to the creation of the Environmental Protection Agency.

When the Electra crashed, it spread over Winthrop Harbor materials akin to what fueled the Cuyahoga River fires: oil and floating debris—except that the debris included living and dead victims, and there were also hundreds of rescuers in, on, and around the water. At the height of rescue and recovery operations, the harbor was filled with 200 mostly wooden craft, 150 skin divers, and hundreds of rescuers neck-deep in seawater, their feet slogging through deep mud and entwining eel grass. They were in no position to flee a fast-flowing jet-fuel fire.

Bill Hollick, former Director of Training at the Massachusetts Fire-fighting Academy, reported to the author that, given the potential of a rapidly moving jet-fuel fire, "the danger to anything afloat and anything along the shoreline would have been phenomenal." "One mitigating factor," he added, "would have been that as the fire burned, the fuel itself would have been consumed. In other words, the fire would have been able to spread only over a finite area before edges of the fuel spill were consumed by the flames." But people, boats, docks, homes—anything flammable—would have been in danger. The 9/11 terrorists selected airliners recently topped up with tens of thousands of pounds of jet fuel to deliver momentary, intense, destructive heat, sufficient to melt a steel structure and bring down the Twin Towers. The intensity of jet-fuel fire was also evident eight years after the Electra crash, in what remains New Hampshire's worst air disaster. Donald Mahler of the *Valley News* of West Lebanon, New Hampshire, recounted events on the fortieth anniversary of the crash. On October 25, 1968, a Northeast Airlines Fairchild-Hiller FH 227C twin turboprop, descending too low in fog toward Lebanon Airport, plowed into Moose Mountain; thirty-two of the forty-two people on board were killed, including the pilot and copilot. The National Transportation Safety Board found that the navigation system in the area may have given off false readings, causing even the plane's experienced pilot to descend prematurely. The forward section disintegrated, but ten people escaped from the tail section, which had broken off and gotten stuck in the trees (tail sections seem to have a life of their own). Once on the ground, survivors were forced to move further down the steep mountain to avoid a fire fed by jet fuel—its heat so intense that a quarter-century later, the pilot's son noted the coloration of rocks at the site made them look "almost as if they were fired in a kiln," Mahler reports. A member of the National Guard vividly recalled decades later: "The main part of the plane was just melted from the heat and it ran like little rivers of aluminum down the mountain."

Luckily, there was no lake of fire on Winthrop Harbor on the evening of October 4, 1960. Perhaps the fact that the surface temperature of the early autumn water was in the low 60s added an element of safety. But even so that small bay surely seemed like a stretch of hell, with the smell of paraffin in the air and bodies everywhere, bumping up against the rocks at the end of Runway 9 and entombed in the wrecked fuselage below. "They looked like dolls," reported one scuba diver after peering through the murky water at dead passengers strapped in their seats.

When the Masones came ashore with the first survivor, awaiting them was Dr. Joseph Gregory, of Bartlett Parkway in Winthrop, who had heard the crash and gone straight to the beach with his medical bag in hand. Gregory determined that the man had two broken legs and possibly a fractured skull. The doctor ministered to the survivor as best he could, giving the man an injection—probably morphine—

to ease the pain and laying him upon the clam flats to await ambulances whose sirens now rent the evening air.

Through his marine glasses, as he called them, a Winthrop police officer had seen victims swimming in the water and seven or eight boats trying to pick them up. The officer stepped up to an arriving fire truck and told the driver to "call for all available ambulances."

Jim Masone's dad decided to remain on the beach to help with victims being brought ashore. Jim took his boat back out to search for survivors, as he did repeatedly that evening.

Don Regan, a commander in the U.S. Naval Reserve, actually saw the crash, tossed his kayak into the water, and paddled to the crash site. He quickly recognized what was going on: gravely injured passengers, still belted into their seats, were being tipped back by their own weight, causing their heads to submerge. Passengers were drowning in their seats. Regan also identified the pattern of crash injuries, later confirmed by the CAB: head gashes, heavy bleeding, and broken legs.

Regan edged his kayak alongside the floating bodies and, using his paddle as a tool, he moved them toward bigger boats, where they could be pulled aboard. Eventually he abandoned his kayak and began to work with rescuers on the larger craft. "We tried first to get to everyone who seemed alive," he said.

As the rescuers worked, the fading October light, after sunset, shifted the crimson sky toward amethyst, a deep purple, and the final indigo of night. All around the harbor, Ed McGrath could see vehicles "form a chain of lights, a brilliant necklace reaching across the runways to the muddy shore."

A radio and television call for skin divers had brought a hundred and fifty or more, and the divers were the first affected by the dying of the light as it no longer reached below the surface. Still, as *Time* reported, "none hesitated to thrash through black, blinding water while boat propellers churned around them." Whirring propellers are a profound danger to divers. In the glory days of the sponge diving industry in the Gulf of Mexico, more divers were killed by propellers than by any other cause.

When Martin Rogers, a twenty-eight-year-old from Marblehead, heard the crash, he was at the Cottage Park Yacht Club. He and his friend Dick Fulham ran to the nearest rowboat, jumped in, and paddled to the crash site. They saw a stewardess swimming and pointed their boat toward her.

"That stewardess was the bravest girl I ever saw," Rogers reported. "She told us not to help her, but to help a man clinging to the last visible part of the plane. While I balanced the boat, Fulham went to pull her in. 'Never mind me. Get that man over there on the piece of plane,' she said. We went for him. He was in pretty bad shape." After pulling him on board, they returned to the stewardess, clinging to the mooring rope of a pleasure boat, shivering and terribly upset. Despite her shock and personal danger, she was true to her training and put the rescue of passengers first.

At the instant the Lockheed Electra struck the 10,000 to 20,000 starlings, United Airlines, then calling itself the nation's number one airline, was interviewing at its office on Stuart Street in downtown Boston for the still new and glamorous profession of airline stewardess: to be hired, you had to be female, at least twenty years old, and a high-school graduate. What was it like, one wonders, to walk out of an interview into the October twilight and hear news of Boston's first air disaster? Paul Benzaquin—the respected host of a Boston radio talk show, who a year earlier had published a book about the Cocoanut Grove fire—came on the air, his highly recognizable voice grave:

> This is Paul Benzaquin. An Eastern Airlines Electra has crashed at Winthrop Beach. Firemen, policemen, civil defense, civil defense auxiliary, and other civilian rescuers are still bringing in the grim stretchers, now covered over with blankets, their victims beyond all hope. The scene along this beach grows more tragic with every moment. A Coast Guard helicopter hovers fifty feet above the water, with a light at its wheel base so that it can help light the grim work carried on by the rescuers below. The debris is being pulled away. The tide is moving in on the beach. It is difficult for all of the rescuers to work. Slowly, lighting plants are being installed. A portable generator has been mounted on the beach in the long and painful search for bodies.

John Phelan, twenty-six, was sitting in his Bellevue Terrace home when he heard what sounded to him like two simultaneous explosions—"like jets breaking the sound barrier": "I ran outside and saw the tail of the plane floating. I grabbed my flippers—I'm a skin diver—and ran to the water's edge." Phelan could see four or five people floating, but he was unable to tell if they were dead or alive. Stan Cooper, his neighbor, was already returning to shore with his boat and a body in it. The two went back out together and reached six more victims—all but two dead. Phelan said: "We brought them in to the beach and left them." Those alive had head wounds—one had a terrible gash and was unconscious; the other was mumbling that he was on his way to Greenville when the plane "had flown through a big flight of sea gulls." Cooper and Phelan pulled another man from the water whom they took to be a crew member, at least at that time still alive.

By now the tail section had begun to drift on the incoming tide, toyed with by the currents, moving a hundred yards or more from where the plane had punched into the bay minutes earlier—six to eight dead passengers visible to rescuers now paddling around the wreckage in motley craft, peering inside, looking for anyone left alive. On one of Jim Masone's trips into the harbor, the eighteen-year-old paddled over to the tail and lifted up a piece of crushed metal with his oar to see if there was anyone alive. He tugged at a leg, "and that's all it was"—the rest of the body was nowhere in sight. An arriving physician, Louis Schraffa, went out to the aircraft wreckage himself to scrutinize it, but found only the dead inside.

That evening Jim Masone made many trips from shore to bay and back again, carrying the living and dead amid a fast-changing crash scene; not surprisingly, the timeless sea is also a restless sea. "The stuff was floating away fast," Jim told the *Globe*. Riding the eddies and currents, the debris was scattering: clothing, baggage, pocketbooks, mail, floating bodies—even an empty yellow life raft bobbing amid the flotsam and jetsam.

"Soon there didn't seem to be anyone left alive," Jim remembered. "The helicopters were only interested in survivors. When they hovered overhead, we signaled thumbs-up for alive, thumbs-down for dead." Too quickly, Jim realized, all the living had been rescued.

Perhaps the most dramatic rescue of the evening was that of Albert H. Nordin, a nineteen-year-old Marine Corps recruit from Whitman, Massachusetts, and a skin-diving enthusiast. As the Electra took off from Runway 9 to carry him toward Parris Island and his new future, he was seated aft of one of the wings. Everything happened so quickly that Albert never even learned the name of the Marine recruit sitting next to him. As he recalled:

> The takeoff seemed smooth, and I looked out the window as we flew over the bay. Then the plane took a sudden turn. It seemed like it was being turned around. Then it fell. The next thing I knew we were in the water. I managed to push out the porthole and squirm through. I started to swim. I was covered with oil. Before I got far, I passed out.

After Albert blacked out, Winthrop residents were able to reach him and drag him to safety. When Albert's parents learned of the crash, they were sure their son was dead until reporters called at 7:30 p.m. to tell them that he had escaped. "Life was suddenly good again for Mr. and Mrs. Nordin," wrote one of the newsmen. The Nordins rushed to Winthrop Community Hospital, less than a mile from the crash scene. They found Albert being treated for a broken leg. "He was sitting there, waiting for us," they told the *Globe*. "The doctors told us he was the luckiest person on the plane."

One of the first public safety officers to arrive at the crash site was Captain Charles W. Wood of the Winthrop Fire Department. "When the first call came to the station," he wrote in the *Globe*, "we hitched an engine to our motor launch and sped to the waterfront. I could see the tail of the plane still out of the water and a few people struggling in the water." The launch arrived at the floating wreckage just as the first civilians reached it from the yacht club.

Wood reported:

> We pulled out one girl from the water. She was wearing a uniform and I think she was a stewardess. Then we hauled a marine into the boat. Both were alive. Our boat was small. We spotted what looked like an officer of the plane. We pulled him in and headed for the shore. The marine and the stewardess walked up the pier and were helped into an ambulance. The officer was unconscious. We had to carry him.

Wood took his launch back out to the crash scene. By now dead passengers, strapped to their seats, had begun to pop to the surface from the main section of the Electra, lying on the bottom of the bay. The phenomenon created moments of surreal surprise as rescuers worked furiously against the vanishing light. Dead passengers, strapped in their seats, loomed up and out of the water, as if in a scene from the twisted imagination of a Hollywood horror film director.

Walter Baker, a fifty-six-year-old resident of Winthrop, owned one of the first civilian powerboats to arrive at the crash site; his boat was routinely kept at the Cottage Park Yacht Club. He navigated carefully among the floating dead to reach two living passengers. Other rescuers—including many tawny-haired boys whose geometry homework lay interrupted at home—used oars as tools to gently brush aside the dead so as to reach the living. Here and there they found a dual floating seat: a husband and wife seated side by side in death as in life.

Baker picked up an elderly man with a bad head injury; he had been bound for Charlotte, North Carolina, he reported. Among the rescued who were still conscious, one of the first things uttered was the passenger's intended destination—as if, while reading their newspaper or a favorite Bible passage, some navigational error had wrongly placed them in Winthrop Harbor, or they had gotten off at the wrong subway stop— alighting perhaps at nearby Revere Beach Amusement Park, and now viewing themselves in the bent reality of a funhouse mirror.

Baker gathered up one survivor and three dead; there were "bodies floating everywhere," he recalled. His boat filled to capacity with tragic cargo, he puttered shoreward. Piteously few brought in were alive, and most of those were unconscious. While some boats, like Baker's, got to bring in the living, even if among the dead, most boats that day carried only the dead or, worse still, body parts of the dead. That day the brave boatmen of Winthrop Harbor resembled Charon of ancient myth, whose job it was to ferry souls of the newly dead across the River Styx from the world of the living to the underworld.

With the crash occurring at low tide, up to 200 yards of mud flats lay between the Winthrop residents arriving on foot and the water's edge. After slogging through the mud to reach the water, rescuers still had to deal with mud underfoot as they strove to reach living victims to save them from drowning. Housewives, who had abandoned supper-time kitchens to rush to the water to see what had happened, realized a special need and rushed home to fetch blankets to cover soaked victims, many in medical shock. Other blankets were used to drape the dead being brought to shore in increasing numbers and laid upon the flats or lined up neatly on a beached raft, awaiting the ambulances then fighting their way toward the shore through traffic on the town's two main access roads.

The Cottage Park Yacht Club, at this time, was the epicenter of rescue and recovery efforts. Even though Logan had 360 planes that took off and landed daily at an airfield that jutted dramatically seaward, it had no water rescue plan. At that time such a plan was not required. Thirty-seven years of fatality-free operations can create laxity, the kind of laxity that can be fatal.

"It looked pathetic," Mrs. Masone told the *Globe*: "You could see all the rescue equipment across at the airport. They were useless. Everything was over here and they are at the airport, and didn't seem to have any boats."

Jim Masone said of the people he fetched out of the bay that evening: "I think one was the copilot." The man "was incoherent. He kept saying, 'I have to get to Greenland.'" Surely, shock and severe injury had twisted Greenville to Greenland in the man's mind. When the Electra struck the bay, the nose and left wing took the full force of deceleration. It was amazing the copilot had anything to say, since he would soon die, as sadly would all the fine flight deck crew on Eastern 375. With their deaths, any firsthand account of what happened in the cockpit was lost forever.

Another rescue boat appeared to have picked up the pilot, with a helicopter airlifting him by basket from the boat to Logan, where an ambulance sped him to the hospital. But Captain Curtis W. Fitts, copilot Martin J. Calloway, and flight engineer Malcolm Hall were all killed after a brief, valiant struggle to save their plane and its passengers.

From Jim's boat he could see other boats "bringing girls into shore" and rescue trucks and ambulances spreading across the beach: "Everyone seemed to be trying to help. People were taking off their coats and shirts to cover those hurt."

One man was so hurt, Jim reported, that "we couldn't lift him into the boat. We tied a rope under his arms and towed him to a boat with a winch. They hoisted him out. A helicopter took him."

When he realized there were no more to rescue, Jim Masone switched from rescue to recovery, as did others in small boats. In the gathering darkness, Jim began to gather the dead, still floating in their seats: "We tied them together and towed them to land." The civilian rescuers included the Milano brothers of Hermon Street—Walter, twenty, and Donald, fifteen—who between them brought twenty bodies to shore.

As one observer noted in the *Globe*: "Youngsters in the small boats did a wonderful job rescuing people and bringing bodies to shore. . . . All along a quarter-mile length of seawall, bodies were being ferried in, laid on the mud until police could carry them away. The kids deserve a big hand for what they did."

William Carabine, a Winthrop auxiliary police officer, had been standing on Bellevue Street on a hill overlooking the harbor and saw the plane crash. He rushed to the beach and saw two double seats from the plane floating with passengers in them. "I gained a rope and sort of lassoed the seats and pulled them into shore," he wrote in the *Globe*. The four were dead. With help, he removed them from their seats and took them to the East Boston Relief Hospital.

Among first to reach the beach were Rev. William Francis—nephew to Richard Cardinal Cushing of Boston, who three months later would deliver the invocation at the inauguration of President John F. Kennedy—and Rev. William McCarthy, both of St. Rose Church in Winthrop. They gave last rites to those they found on the Winthrop shore, even as priests from Our Lady of the Airways Chapel gave last rites to the dead retrieved from the bay at the end of Runway 9.

Two Boston police officers, Daniel Fallon and Stephen Gaffney, arrived from Brighton by ambulance; together they brought in twelve bodies found amid floating debris, before finding even one person alive. That man was revived by Fallon and Gaffney with artificial respiration and taken to Winthrop Community Hospital.

Amid the understandable chaos and confusion of the scene, one survivor was mistaken for dead. As reported by *Time*, "Civil Defense Director Jerry Wyman uncovered a blanketed body, applied a resuscitator, and brought one 'dead man' to life."

Into the Bosom of Abraham

The Duke of Wellington, who defeated Napoleon at the battle of Waterloo, is supposed to have said that "the battle of Waterloo was won on the playing fields of Eton," suggesting British officers had acquired their keen battle skills at Eton and other elite schools for the English upper class. Others, more democratically disposed, contended that Waterloo was won on common village playing fields all across Shakespeare's sceptered isle, for it was on such fields that average boys learned the skills, competitive spirit, and resourcefulness that was widely and beneficially dispersed among the British troops in the Napoleonic wars. In similar fashion, boating skills had been widely and beneficially dispersed among Winthrop's citizens when the Electra fell out of the October sky and into their bay.

Interestingly, when Alan Boyd of the CAB said that the crash of Eastern 375 "was not what is called a survivable crash," he did not explain why ten people did survive. The CAB was mandated to find out why an air crash occurred and to recommend steps to make planes and the air transportation system safer, based on what they learned. The CAB was not asked to judge the skill set or heroism of the random citizens who responded after a crash. That judgment was left to others.

While the Electra was so ill-starred as to fall from the sky on takeoff in a nonsurvivable crash in thirty feet of water, in one significant sense it fell straight into the bosom of Abraham. If you were going to be on an airliner that crashed into a bay seconds after liftoff, you could not have chosen a better bay for the experience than Winthrop Harbor.

Winthrop is no ordinary town. As on the village fields of England—Shakespeare's "precious stone set in the silver sea"—average boys growing up around Winthrop Harbor acquired keen skills and resourcefulness under the guise of play: in this case, skills in handling small boats and a resourcefulness in dealing with the sea.

Winthrop is tiny: a mere 1.6 square miles circumscribed by seven miles of coastline. Even Euclid might ruin sheets of paper before finally managing to draw a geometric figure that fits those dimensions. Jeffrey Rounds describes the town in "Sylvia Plath and Winthrop-by-the Sea," his essay about the Pulitzer Prize–winning poet, novelist, and short-story writer who lived in Winthrop for much of her childhood: "Approached from the north along the coastal highway, the town sits perched on a rise like a fairy castle . . . it seems so tiny and perfect it might fit in a teacup." And, as the narrator in one of Plath's stories—surely the author herself—reflects: "The sea was something we knew about. Terminus of almost every street, it buckled and swashed and tossed, out of its gray formlessness, china plates, wooden monkeys, elegant shells and dead men's shoes. Wet salt winds raked our playgrounds endlessly."

Winthrop is a peninsula almost by technicality; in the geographer's standard usage, it is more of an island. It is nearly surrounded by water: on one side joined to East Boston by a vital bridge over water; on the other, joined to Revere by a hundred-yard strip of land. If not actually an island, Winthrop is island-like, both in fact and in culture.

Eighteen thousand people lived in Winthrop in 1960, many of them raised with an islander's conscious and unconscious preoccupation with the sea, especially those who grew up before 1950. They had a love-hate relationship with Logan Airport, west of the town across a small bay. Here is a sense of the affectionate side of that relationship seen through the eyes of Sylvia Plath as little girl, as recounted by Paul Alexander in his biography of her:

> For more hours than usual, Sylvia would sit in her room and study the airplanes landing and taking off at Logan, Boston's municipal airport, located across the harbor from Winthrop and in full view from Sylvia's bedroom window. "I marveled at the moving beacons on the runway and watched, until it grew completely dark, the flashing red and green lights that rose and set in the sky like shooting stars," comments a narrator of a short story Plath would one day write. "The airport was my Mecca, my Jerusalem. All night I would dream of flying."

In 1959, after long absence, Sylvia Plath returned to Winthrop to visit the grave of her father, who had died nineteen years earlier, her first and only visit after she moved away from the town. It was a deeply painful experience that she wrote of in the same year in a famous poem eerily called "Electra on Azalea Path." Her father's modest grave marker was on Azalea Path in Winthrop Cemetery. She wrote about it one year before the Electra crashed into Winthrop Bay.

If one studies the geography of Winthrop, and the culture and skill set of many residents that derive from that geography, the swift and sure response of residents when a plane crashed in the bay becomes understandable: "Come on, Dad! Let's go!" We see a community with boat and seaside skills widely dispersed among its population and a tradition of citizen involvement in public safety. Numerous Winthrop residents served as auxiliary police or auxiliary civil defense aides, as might be true on an island where people often perform multiple duties out of necessity. All around the world, island people are resourceful people.

Winthrop citizens were accustomed to acting on their own in the face of calamity without awaiting a full, official response from the municipality. They acted instinctively, as if from the imperative of Leviticus: "Thou shall not stand idly by while your neighbor's blood is shed."

Amazingly, a year after the Electra crash, on September 24, 1961, Winthrop citizens in small boats were again called upon to perform rescue functions for a crashed airliner at Logan. An American Airlines Boeing 707, inbound from San Francisco in the fog, tried to land at Logan on a Sunday morning, overshot the runway, and skidded 400 feet before coming to rest in 8 feet of water in Winthrop Harbor. Remarkably, only three or four aboard the flight incurred even minor injuries, but one man helping in the rescue died of a heart attack. Seventy-one passengers and crew were rescued, not by Logan officials, but by Logan's "auxiliary rescue force": the good citizens of Winthrop.

Winthrop is so like an island that few come to the town unless they live there, have business there, are visiting someone there, or, especially in an earlier time, are spending a summer vacation there—renting on ocean-side streets with names that evoke Miami Beach: Dolphin, Pearl, Wave, Sea Foam, Trident, Coral, Mermaid, and Neptune. Before acquiring property in Hyannisport and Palm Beach, even the

Kennedys of Massachusetts vacationed in Winthrop. The relative self-containment of Winthrop is probably one reason the town has one of the lowest crime rates in Massachusetts.

Everyone in Winthrop grows up within scent of the sea and with sightlines to it. As Sylvia Plath's narrator in the story "Ocean 1212-W" says: "My childhood landscape was not land but the end of the land—the cold, salt, running hills of the Atlantic. I sometimes think my vision of the sea is the clearest thing I own."

In good weather, numbers of Winthrop residents are usually on the water, taking boats out from the Winthrop Yacht Club or the Cottage Park Yacht Club, or hauling their way back in to safe haven in Winthrop. Or they are fussing with boats: putting boats into the water, taking boats out of the water, applying a fresh coat of spar paint, adjusting rigging. Or heading to fish off "the bank" (Georges Bank). Or spending hours talking about seaside matters. While near the harbor master's office, I heard this remark as one man worked on his boat engine, helped by another man whose own boat sat nearby on a boat trailer: "I was out this morning in the harbor and I caught a nine-pound cod. I just came back from three days on the bank, and I could find no cod." The two shared a good chuckle, and, more important, a connection with each other and with the sea. Winthrop sport fishermen, in good weather or bad, can be found surfcasting from a sandy beach onto "the cold, salt, running hills of the Atlantic," surely clarifying their vision of the sea while so doing, making sure it "is the clearest thing I own."

Winthrop bravely pushes far out into Boston Harbor, more so since the Great Hurricane of 1938, New England's worst recorded storm. Coinciding with highest astronomical tides of the year, the hurricane drove a storm surge of twelve to fifteen feet into coastal areas of southern New England. Shirley Gut, the narrow channel that had separated Winthrop from Deer Island, suddenly was filled in by silt. For local seafarers, Shirley Gut had long been the back way out of Boston Harbor to the open Atlantic. There is a wonderful though unsubstantiated story that the USS *Constitution*, after engaging the British in Boston Harbor, flew to the trackless Atlantic through Shirley Gut. After the Hurricane of 1938, the Army Corps of Engineers converted siltedin Shirley Gut into a permanent causeway that connects Winthrop to Deer Island.

Today, the Seaside Striders Running Club as well as casual joggers, bikers, and walkers from Winthrop and surrounding communities use Deer Island's attractive pathways to exercise by the ocean. Deer Island is also home to a sewage treatment plant, located on the former site of the prison from which Bartholomew Flynn, the corrections officer, watched the Electra dive to destruction. While Deer Island belongs to Boston, one can get there by land only by traveling through Winthrop; topographically, at least, Deer Island is now part of Winthrop's long reach seaward, offering some of the most spectacular ocean views on the Atlantic seaboard.

Such is the character of Winthrop, where all summer-long boys and girls played in the water and in boats in the shelter of Winthrop Harbor. In 1960, given the attitudes of the times, far more boys than girls would have been in the boats.

The poet and playwright George Murphy, who grew up in Winthrop in the 1950s, wrote and performs a brilliant monologue, "Electra or the Birds of Death and the Mongoloid Troubadour," which includes a fictionalized account of the 1960 Electra crash.

The central idea of the monologue is that in the summer of 1960 George and his friend, both eleven, desperately want to win a sailboat race in their loved, shared, and not at all sleek New England runabout. A series of bizarre, fascinating, and tragic occurrences block the boys from getting onto the water, but, as consolation at summer's end, they joyously sail forth from the Cottage Park Yacht Club, beyond Winthrop Harbor, for a day of fun and adventure among the many islands of Boston Harbor. In late afternoon, as they return from their perfect day, they watch the Electra plummet into Winthrop Harbor and hell and horror descend upon their bay.

In the monologue, Murphy gives a wonderful example of inventive boat play on Winthrop Harbor, as regularly practiced by local boys, when he and his friend engage in runway surfing. Winthrop boys would position their boats, sails luffing, at the end of Runway 9, facing due east—the very heading of Eastern 375. As outgoing airliners took off, the boys' boat sails would billow as they caught the downdraft, and they would fly across the bay at high speed toward Snake Island. "This was like the Indy 500!" Murphy recalls with exultation, fifty years later. Winthrop boys would repeat this activity fifteen or twenty times a day. For these boys, as for Sylvia Plath, Logan Airport was their Mecca and Jerusalem too—complete with dreams of flying.

Watching such antics, what adult would think that resourcefulness, inventiveness, and vital skills were being acquired by aimless play, or that these qualities and skills might save lives when an airliner plunged into Winthrop Bay? Here is a tiny example of off-the-water resourcefulness: before ambulances were able to reach the Winthrop shore with stretchers, civilians lashed oars together to create litters to ferry victims across the hazardous mud flats and down side streets to waiting rescue vehicles.

John F. Kennedy, who so loved the sea, was one of those young East Coast yachtsmen the U.S. Navy eagerly sought to skipper PT boats darting among South Sea islands in World War II. These were young men comfortable around boats and bays, having earned that comfort through summer boat and water play, just like the boys of Winthrop. Kennedy's skills with boats and as a swimmer would make him a hero in the South Pacific and help to launch his political career. His kinship with the sea was revealed in eloquent remarks delivered at the America's Cup Race in 1962. Kennedy watched the race aboard the USS *Joseph P. Kennedy Jr.*, named for his older brother, who had been killed in the war and with whom as a teammate he had raced in sailboat regattas, with JFK as the youthful skipper.

I really don't know why it is that all of us are so committed to the sea, except that I think, in addition to the fact that the sea changes, and the light changes, and ships change, it's because we all came from the sea. And it is an interesting biological fact that all of us have in our veins the exact same percentage of salt in our blood that exists in the ocean, and, therefore, we have salt in our blood, in our sweat, in our tears. We are tied to the ocean. And when we go back to the sea, whether it is to sail or to watch it, we are going back from whence we came.

"I have been interested in the sea from my earliest boyhood," Kennedy once said. On his fifteenth birthday, his parents gave him a nine-meter wooden sailboat, *Victura*, which now keeps vigil outside the Kennedy Library on Boston Harbor, its bow facing the horizon, awaiting the return of the boy who sailed her. Even during the Cuban missile crisis, President Kennedy, doodling, sketched pictures of the *Victura*. Many boys in Winthrop shared Kennedy's love of the sea, fondness for boats, and skills that would make them heroes. For example, on that awful October day, fourteen-year-old Peter Smith raced from his shoreline home on Bartlett Parkway to the yacht club float. Peter and a man leaped into a fourteen-foot tender and rowed to the crash scene, their oars flashing in the crimson light of sunset, even as they brushed past the floating dead. Ed McGrath wrote of how the two rescued a victim who had fallen back into the water from a small boat onto which he had desperately clung, a deep gash suffered in the fall leaving him unconscious.

"Boy and man also struggled to pull a second victim into the small craft. Water-soaked clothing created excess weight and the boat almost capsized," McGrath reported. The two rowed back toward the mud flats with their victims, "horrified, sickened by the sight of heads bobbing in the water along their course." Other rescuers had found two men hanging onto a yacht mooring line, and another man with his head "savagely gashed," but still having strength enough to hang onto floating debris.

In their quick use of their deft boat skills, despite personal danger, the Winthrop responders evoke memories of the all-volunteer U.S. Life-Saving Service. These were young men who carried out sea rescues at danger points along the coastline from 1848 until the founding of the Coast Guard in 1915. Their grave markers or—for those whose bodies were lost to the pounding surf—their names etched upon cenotaphs can be found still, close by the pitiless sea.

"Hub's Biggest Rescue Mobilization"
Minutes after the plane crash, Boston's Mayor John Collins interrupted a brief vacation to Bermuda to direct all city departments to offer "whatever aid and assistance possible" to the victims of Eastern 375. By 6:30 p.m., forty minutes after the crash, Collins had already talked with Deputy Mayor John McMorrow and ordered him to divert

fire, rescue, and civil defense equipment to the crash scene, saying that he would return to Boston that night. Collins knew suffering; he and four of his children had been stricken with polio in the 1950s. While all his children were to recover, Collins himself was confined to a wheelchair. By dint of his affliction and progressive politics, Collins evoked the hallowed memory of none other than Franklin Delano Roosevelt when residents entered the voting booths in heavily Democratic Boston.

From 1960 to 1968, Collins revitalized Boston. The city had prospered greatly during World War II as the major U.S. port closest to the European theater, but after the war, the city's economic life had fallen into torpor. The mayor and Edward J. Logue, the visionary head of Boston's Redevelopment Authority, mapped out a plan for creation of "the New Boston," which included $90 million for urban renewal and a push to expand Logan Airport. Collins and Logue dreamed of a Boston that would be the epicenter of New England's technology future, with an expanded Logan pumping lifeblood into the region's commerce.

By the late 1950s, New England's economic future had begun to brighten once again. On October 4, 1957, precisely three years before the Electra crash, the A-flat beep of *Sputnik* was heard over the United States for the first time, then again every ninety-six minutes. News of the Soviet Union's launching of *Sputnik* had sent a shock wave across the United States and led to a dramatic boost in federal spending on defense technologies and education, which augured well for New England and for Boston, the so-called Athens of America.

Historically, New England has played a crucial role in the nation's defense industry. America's first jet engine was built in 1942 at GE in Lynn, Massachusetts, and, in 1960, two of the three top manufacturers of jet engines in the world were in New England: GE in Lynn, and Pratt & Whitney in Hartford, Connecticut. Sikorsky Aircraft in Stratford, Connecticut, was blazing the trail in helicopter development and production. The nation's nuclear submarine fleet was being built and launched in Groton, Connecticut, and Portsmouth, New Hampshire. Itek of Massachusetts had developed the high-altitude photography for the U-2 spy plane. MIT's federally funded Lincoln Laboratory spun out ideas in electronics that quickly gave rise to new technology firms sprouting up along Route 128, which ringed Boston.

The Chief Gate

Logan International Airport was to be the chief gate for those entering and leaving New England in the jet age, one reason news of the Electra's crash came as such a shock to Boston. Added to the shock was embarrassment that a few hundred yards off the end of Runway 9 lay a wrecked jet turboprop under seawater, whose survivors had been rescued, in good part, by boys from Winthrop in small boats, while Logan officials looked on helplessly. And, on the bottom of the bay, lay contracts for a new missile system, involving two nations, and the dead engineer who had carried them. Not a good omen for a revivified regional economy, led by a New Boston, queen of technology cities. Thus it was no surprise that Mayor Collins quickly boarded a plane for home and left behind the blue-green waters of Bermuda.

Shortly before 6:00 p.m., the Boston Fire Department sounded its disaster call, and ten police ambulances and eight patrol cars were sent speeding to Winthrop, along with fire and emergency apparatus. Additional details of Boston police, assembled from stations around the city, were dispatched to East Boston and Winthrop. State police took on responsibility for the mobilization of equipment at the end of Runway 9, even as the Coast Guard began to secure Winthrop Harbor.

While Boston Police Deputy Superintendent John J. Danehy oversaw general operations from police headquarters, three other deputies—John J. Slattery Jr., William J. Hogan, and Joseph Cummings—split oversight of operations in the field. The official police report for October 5, 1960, shows Slattery shipping into police storage many objects recovered from the scene, poignantly among them "1 flight officer's overnight bag: brown, dark, zippered, a metal disc marked, C.W. Fitts." By this time, Boston City Hospital had three ambulances en route to the crash scene, and four harbor police boats had swung into Winthrop Harbor. Law enforcement motorized craft joined civilian motorized craft on the bay, although all motorboats proved to have trouble in the shallows—their propellers fouling in the eel grass. Two helicopters were dispatched from the Salem Coast Guard Base, and they began to ferry victims to Logan by basket and return with divers they lowered into the water. As darkness fell, the chopper pilots turned on their search lamps and circled overhead trying to light the crash scene. A third helicopter from Beverly arrived and began to airlift divers to the crash site from the Cottage Park side of the bay.

Radiational cooling quickly turns dry, sunny fall days in New England into chilly nights—especially if you've waded neck-deep into water in street clothes to reach victims. Red Cross disaster units arrived from the Winthrop and greater Boston chapters to offer assistance, both to victims and to a growing number of rescue workers. Two Red Cross disaster trucks, chapter station wagons, and thirty Red Cross workers took up strategic positions along Winthrop beach. They were joined by the Salvation Army and by Winthrop housewives, with their donuts and coffee.

As time passed, the arriving vessels grew bigger. Two thirty-foot Coast Guard cruisers made their way into Winthrop Harbor, along with fireboats, heavy tugs, Coast Guard cutters, and U.S. Navy ships. A Coast Guard buoy tender arrived, as did a massive, 185-foot tender, equipped with two gigantic cranes able to lift airplane wreckage from the floor of the bay. Divers would connect the tail and fuselage sections to cables from the tender, so these sections could be raised and laid upon a barge.

The call for divers had brought to Winthrop Harbor lone civilian skin divers as well as whole dive teams from the Navy, the police and fire departments, and adjacent Revere's Beach City Aqua Knights. Some divers descended into the bay in hard-hat deep-sea diving suits. Others put on wet suits to protect themselves against the cold as the autumn night fell upon coastal New England. The harbor was now alive with circling craft, so many as to present a hazard to each other. Aboard some were police and firefighters equipped with grappling hooks, trying to snag pieces of floating debris and aircraft wreckage. Some wreckage was being transported from the crash scene over to Runway 9 by helicopters using special slings. Searchers were hunting down debris underwater, strewn across the bay, and washed onto shore. But, as one reporter noted, it was often "hard to tell what was debris and what were bodies."

The plan was to work around the clock until all rescue and recovery operations were finished—the living and dead retrieved, all aircraft wreckage and debris gathered.

By now the Federal Bureau of Investigation was on the scene, keeping vigil as divers searched for the locked briefcase with missile-systems documents inside. The FBI agents were easily identifiable. Even sixteen-year-old John Goglia could pick them out: they were the only people aboard the recovery boats who were wearing suits. A car with an FBI driver remained parked on shore, ready to speed off with the sealed briefcase once it was retrieved. The vigil was kept until a Navy lighter—a flat-bottomed cargo boat—hoisted an eight-ton section of the plane from the seafloor; inside was found the briefcase that had been carried by John Wright of King of Prussia, Pennsylvania, an engineer from the research division of the Burroughs Corporation.

Also recovered were two mail pouches with 2,500 letters; other mail was retrieved by volunteer skin divers bringing it in from where it had been dispersed across the bay.

In the early stages, the epicenter of rescue and recovery operations was the Cottage Park Yacht Club, a few hundred yards from 92 Johnson Avenue, where Sylvia Plath had nightly watched "the flashing red and green lights that rose and set in the sky like shooting stars." When it became clear that there would be no more survivors and that what remained to do was recover the bodies, debris, and wreckage, the epicenter of operations shifted across the bay to Runway 9. The mustering of land-based equipment and personnel on Runway 9 had, of course, begun within seconds of the plane's going down, when Logan Tower dispatched five crash trucks to the end of the runway.

Boston's Fire Chief John A. Martin, who was in charge of rescue operations for the city's fire department, sent twelve divers to the scene, fire apparatus from East Boston, fire boats, and engine and ladder companies from downtown stations. Martin also put out a call to other communities, and soon rescue units began arriving from Arlington, Belmont, Brookline, Cambridge, Chelsea, Dedham, Everett, Lynn, Malden, Medford, Quincy, Revere, Somerville, and other cities and towns in eastern Massachusetts. There was a huge crowd on the shore now, to watch Boston Assistant Fire Chiefs John Clougherty and

William Terrenzi set up beach operations. The army also sent personnel from Fort Banks, a former coastal artillery post in Winthrop.

Dive operations were overseen by divers James Walton, of Newburyport, and Jim Cahill, of Beverly. It was Walton who had trained young Goglia as a diver and called him right after the crash, asking "Got your gear?" Walton picked Goglia up in a police cruiser and took him to the yacht club, where Goglia put on his gear and got to work. His assignment: to search the shallows for victims. The sights he saw and the body parts he held in his hands as he kicked his flippers and surfaced "put a mark on me," Goglia recalled decades later. (I met John Goglia after he retired from the NTSB and had three lengthy interviews with him. Unless otherwise noted, those interviews are the sources of his quotations and comments in this book.)

During the recovery phase, divers could not readily see if additional bodies remained inside the main section of the sunken aircraft. The fuselage lay in murky water, and the divers could not easily get inside, as jagged metal effectively sealed off both ends. Walton and Cahill described the plane's fuselage as looking as if it had been "ripped open with a can opener" and the cockpit as being "smashed in." Two key parts of the aircraft were never recovered: the windshield and the two pitot tubes, instruments through which air flows to give pilots vital airspeed readings. In retrospect, both were probably a casualty of the encounter with 10,000 to 20,000 birds and then a direct hit upon the bay as the plane crashed.

Charles Tarbi, who had ably covered East Boston and Winthrop over the years for *The Boston Globe*, was uncharacteristically late to report on this important story. Winthrop Patrolman Robert Crawford had pressed Tarbi into service to help remove parked cars blocking the arrival of emergency vehicles, and to divert mindless sightseers' traffic. Tarbi, Crawford, and four passersby pushed a dozen vehicles up onto Cottage Park sidewalks. While they were doing so, two police officers were seen carrying a victim nearly a full block to a waiting ambulance. Boston police soon blocked off road access between East Boston and Winthrop via Saratoga Street, and Revere police blocked off access to Winthrop via Short Beach, their joint action preventing curious motorists from getting anywhere near the crash scene.

After the plane struck the bay, survivors were seen swimming or clinging to mooring lines. Observers noted that no shouts could be heard on shore; those alive seemed "calm." Of course, they were not calm in any traditional sense. Those left alive were in medical shock, some of them moribund; those better off, who were able to swim, were surely in a shocked psychological state. Almost all survivors reported having "blacked out," either before or after the crash.

Among citizens quick to aid in the rescue were people who had gone to the Cottage Park Yacht Club to enjoy the precious late afternoon October sunshine after a rainy September and with November looming ahead, with its premonitions of winter. "There is a certain slant of light on winter afternoons that hangs like cathedral tunes," wrote Emily Dickinson, the belle of Amherst, Massachusetts. New Englanders know how important it is to gather up October sunshine, with its last traces of summer. Arthur Johnson, Dick Fulham, and Jack O'Brien were at the club when they heard the crash and dashed out of harbor-side relaxation into rescue action when they realized the unthinkable had happened: a giant airliner had crashed into their bay.

Following the actions of first civilian responders, an array of second-stage responses began. The crash scene became a blend of the heroic and the surreal.

State Civil Defense Department officials arrived along with fire companies, state troopers by the hundreds, and Massachusetts District Commission Police. Even the Massachusetts Department of Motor Vehicles sent a detail to deal with the clogged Winthrop streets. Meanwhile, on the beach, stark urgency reigned, as captured by Ed McGrath: "Firemen shouted near-hysterical when they saw a glimmer of hope, 'Get more oxygen. For God's sake get some more here.'"

"Hospital Staffs Rally to Aid Crash Victims"
Hospitals in Winthrop and Boston went on emergency alert when news came of the crash. Off-duty nurses were recalled to Winthrop Community Hospital, and cots were lined up along the hospital corridors. With severe trauma often comes medical shock and a need for transfusions. Lawrence Memorial Hospital in Medford dispatched blood plasma by taxi to augment supplies already en route to Win-

throp Hospital from the Red Cross. The Massachusetts Regional Blood Center, on Dartmouth Street in Boston, shipped whole blood to Winthrop Hospital. Offers of blood came in from Boston's Massachusetts General Hospital (known as Mass General or MGH), which had the largest supply of any hospital in the region, Whidden Memorial Hospital in Everett, and the Chelsea Naval Hospital. Physicians and nurses at the East Boston Relief Station, Boston City Hospital, and MGH readied to receive victims, with doctors and nurses asked to report for duty and emergency equipment set in place.

"Three hospitals and the East Boston Relief Station received living victims of the crash with quickly mobilized staffs," wrote Frances Burns of *The Boston Globe* under the headline "Hospital Staffs Rally to Aid Crash Victims."

The sixty-five-bed Winthrop Community Hospital, less than a mile from the crash site, dispatched the first ambulances and received the first victims: eleven survivors were brought there by ambulance or private car, two dying soon after arrival. Of the nine still alive by late night, four were in critical condition and five in serious condition. Since the hospital kept only a small supply of blood on hand, hospital staff, under the direction of Dr. John Collins, the temporary chief of staff, called for and received additional supplies. As it turned out, the initial supply available proved sufficient because of the small number of survivors. As Edna Price, a Winthrop Hospital administrator, wearily told Frances Burns at midnight, "The staff was wonderful. We could have cared for more."

Victims taken to the East Boston Relief Station were saturated "with kerosene-smelling fuel oil," reported Marie Feudo, the registered nurse in charge of the facility. The station had emergency equipment in place before the first victim arrived, but only one person brought in was still alive: Justin Bauman, forty-two, of Reading, Pennsylvania. Bauman was given first aid and rushed by ambulance to Boston City Hospital, but not before he expressed concern for his friend Henry King, who had been taken to MGH. Bauman remained alive at Boston City Hospital until Saturday, October 8, when he died of multiple injuries, bringing the final death toll from the crash to sixty-two.

When word of the airliner crash reached MGH, doctors and nurses put into effect a prearranged disaster plan. The aptly named Dr. Oliver Cope, an academic surgeon and burn expert, was in charge of the plan. He was making rounds when he heard the news, and he immediately ordered the front doors of the hospital shut, with all departing doctors halted and turned back to the emergency ward.

But only two crash victims were brought to MGH—Justin Bauman's friend Henry King, also of Reading, Pennsylvania, who was dead on arrival, and U.S. Air Force Major Sylvester Koenigs from Greenville, South Carolina, who was stationed at Otis Air Force Base on Cape Cod, in Massachusetts. When Major Koenigs boarded the Electra, he was bound for Greenville, on his way to a temporary assignment in Florida. In the crash, he suffered chest injuries, cuts about his neck, and other possible injuries. At MGH he was placed on the danger list, and his wife was tracked down and notified.

That evening a call came in to MGH from Eastern Airlines officials, offering blood. A former Eastern stewardess, who happened to be in the emergency ward when the victims arrived, also offered to donate blood.

It is an interesting note that MGH's disaster plan came into being after the Cocoanut Grove nightclub fire in 1942. Dr. Earle W. Wilkins, who served as Chief of Emergency Medical Services at MGH from 1968 until 1988, recalls arriving at the hospital the night of the fire, when he was still a medical student, and fully grasping the scope of the catastrophe when he saw a hundred draped bodies lying outside the hospital. The "fire in the Grove" had triggered the creation of the MGH disaster plan implemented by Dr. Cope on the evening of October 4, 1960. While MGH had a plan for handling a medical disaster, there was no coordinated plan of response to a medical disaster on the part of other hospitals in Boston. On the evening of the Electra crash, ad hoc decisions were made in the field by a dizzying array of personnel from federal, state, city, and town agencies, and emergency rescue units— including decisions as to which hospitals victims would be taken.

Right after Dr. Wilkins assumed his post as MGH Chief of Emergency Medical Services in 1968, he was driving in his car when he heard a radio news report that Massachusetts had been ranked forty-eighth out of the fifty states in emergency medical response. Wilkins took upon himself the daunting task of persuading seventeen Boston area teaching hospitals to develop a coordinated response to medical disasters. A key element would be that one person would make all decisions so as to speed effective response and avoid confusion. Responsibility for the decision-making role would rotate among the hospitals, each having a designated, trained team of a physician, nurse, and administrator ready to assume responsibility for regulating the entire system. Thanks to Dr. Wilkins, that plan went into effect in the 1970s.

In 1985, Boston Med Flight—critical-care air transport offered around the clock, seven days a week, without regard for ability to pay—was added to the emergency response armamentarium to reduce premature death and disability. Today, Boston Med Flight uses helicopters and fixed-wing aircraft, strategically sited across Massachusetts, to offer critical care en route to a teaching hospital. At the time of the Electra crash, while helicopters aided heroically in rescue at the crash scene, the gravely injured were offloaded nearby from rescue baskets and taken by ambulance to hospitals along urban roadways crowded with rush-hour traffic.

Sadly, on the evening of October 4, 1960, the central task of area hospitals switched over far too quickly from the task of saving lives to that of identifying the dead and preparing their bodies for release to their loved ones. Temporary morgues had been set up during the height of rescue and recovery operations, but these were transitory stops for the dead. Like so much of modern life, coming into the world and departing from it require official paperwork. The dead brought to temporary morgues—sixteen at Winthrop's police station, ten at the fire station, more at the customs shed at Logan—needed to make one additional stop before being released into their families' loving care. They had to be transferred to a hospital or a morgue so that death could be officially pronounced. In order to die, you need an authorized signature.

The Morgue

A meeting of Harvard Medical School pathologists at the Boston City Hospital morgue had ended shortly after 8:00 p.m. on October 4, just as the first bodies began to arrive. The pathologists were quickly put to work. The bodies came in at a slow rate at first, then more rapidly. At 8:30, fingerprint experts arrived from the Boston Police Department; by this time, police wagons and ambulances were lined up along Massachusetts Avenue, waiting to enter through the morgue's gates. Police hurriedly unloaded the dead, going away with empty stretchers to bring in more. A crowd had begun to gather outside the gates, with the police pushing them back. By 10:00 p.m., forty bodies had been brought in, arriving one to an ambulance in almost all cases.

At 9:30 a man entered the morgue asking if he could identify a body, but he was told by a white-coated attendant that it would be 10:00 before anyone would be admitted for identification purposes. He was shown to the waiting room. It is difficult to imagine a grimmer spot than the waiting room of a morgue on the night of an airliner crash.

The first relatives of a victim to arrive were Mr. and Mrs. James Supple of Needham, Massachusetts. James Supple's seventy-year-old mother, Elsie Supple, of Dorchester, had been flying to see her grandson in Boyertown, Pennsylvania. Elsie Supple's son-in-law, George Ryan, of Dorchester, Massachusetts, also entered the waiting room. He spoke quietly of taking Mrs. Supple to the plane, watching it take off, and then heading home, passing fire apparatus coming in the opposite direction through the Sumner Tunnel. It was two hours before George Ryan learned that his wife's mother had been killed in the crash of Eastern 375. He recollected: "We were going to walk up to the Observation Platform but decided not to."

The waiting room of the morgue began to fill. Shortly after 11:00 p.m., Boston City Hospital's assistant superintendent, Dr. James Sarcchetti, came into the waiting room and read to the fifteen people present the names of thirty-four victims that police and pathologists had been able to identify. He read descriptions of two unidentified victims. As he read the names, tears appeared in the eyes of James Supple's wife. No one in the group of fifteen spoke. They sat in silence.

In Proust's *Remembrance of Things Past*, the narrator bites into a madeleine— a small, rich, shell-shaped cake often decorated with coconut and jam—which evokes a flood of memories that fill 3,000 pages and infuse life into 2,000 characters. Such is the brain's ability to link memory, taste, and smell: vast amounts of emotionally freighted information can be awakened by a fleeting taste or smell, and recalled decades later in what Proust scholars call an "involuntary memory."

For those who had to identify the body of a loved one killed in the crash, the smell of unspent jet fuel and death would be forever yoked together in such an involuntary memory, with the loss of a beloved linked to the unmistakable odor of kerosene. Darting across an alley in Boston's Back Bay or walking the streets of Philadelphia years later, a whiff of kerosene could bring back the night a loved one died in Winthrop Harbor.

Poignancy

After any airliner crash, there are inevitably stories of lives spared by fate. The wings of death sweep low overhead and cast a long shadow, leaving behind a shudder and a chill, but life still goes on, otherwise unaffected. So it was with Eastern 375.

Of the original seventeen marine recruits scheduled to be on Eastern 375, five survived. Three escaped alive from the crash: Albert Nordin, of Whitman; Richard Nix, of Sudbury; and James Reed, of Leominster. Two more missed the flight by chance: James Powlesland and Michael Cordice, both of Portland, Maine, phoned in to report potential difficulty in making the flight, so they were switched to another group of recruits who were leaving later. That group gathered at South Station in Boston and left as the clock struck midnight. Powlesland and Cordice were alive, even as a dozen recruits from their original group lay dead. That thought and the departure as the clock struck twelve evokes the *frisson* of the first line of George Orwell's 1984: "It was a bright cold day in April, and the clocks were striking thirteen."

Two lifelong buddies from Lowell, Massachusetts, Edward Robinson and Charles Pierce Jr., had enlisted in the Marine Corps under what was called the buddy plan. Both were killed. Two others, George DeMoura and Robert Duarte, of Taunton, Massachusetts, were flying off to boot camp together. Both of them also died; their wakes were held together at the Silva Funeral Home in Taunton.

The Wail of Ambulances

Ed McGrath, who wrote such beautiful, heartfelt prose about the crash, even while against a working reporter's tight deadline, was the de facto poet of the catastrophe in Winthrop Harbor. He captured for our eyes a half-century later, as if in amber, what happens when a passenger airliner striving for Magee's "wind-swept heights with easy grace" instead falls nose first into the merciless sea.

The Greek Nobel Prize–winning poet Odysseus Elytis once wrote: "Poetry begins where death is deprived of the last word." By way of McGrath, we can see how a town, so tiny and perfect it could fit into a teacup, was transformed when a plane taking off from Mecca—or was it Jerusalem?—crashed into its bay.

> Winthrop, a peninsula with only two approaches, was a knot of emergency traffic. Never before were its roads so blocked, and never before had residents gazed from their windows to see lawns covered with ambulances, police and fire vehicles.
>
> Winthrop could count the victims with each mournful wail of an ambulance siren. And Winthrop was awake until the dawn hours— shocked by the toll.

4 The Case of the Boston Electra

We suddenly became cognizant of a large flock or cloud of starlings. These you cannot see from the end of the runway. Or we could not see them before we started out. They were just suddenly there. Starlings are very excitable birds: they wheel and turn in a flock so that one minute, when you are looking at them, you see nothing, and the next minute, as the cloud shifts, there is a big black cloud in front of you.

They hit the front of the airplane, resembling machine gun fire. Just brrrrrummm! There wasn't a square inch of my windshield that wasn't splattered with bird remains. I couldn't see a thing.
—Eastern Airlines Captain W. H. Jenkins

On a bright cold January morning in 1961, the Civil Aeronautics Board began hearings on the crash of the Boston Electra in the auditorium of the Massachusetts Air National Guard, barely a runway from the crash scene. Three months of intensive, mostly behind-the-scenes investigation would now come to public light.

During three days of hearings, CAB investigators would hear from forty-three witnesses and experts. But no testimony—not even that of passengers who survived the horrifying crash into the bay—would be as chilling as that of Captain W. H. Jenkins. Just two weeks after the crash, piloting another Eastern Airlines Electra at Logan, Jenkins was roaring down the takeoff runway, approaching liftoff, when a huge flock of starlings suddenly appeared and hit the entire front of his aircraft like machine-gun fire—even blotting out his view from the cockpit.

Since Jenkins had not yet broken from the ground—and still had sufficient runway ahead to stop his plane—he was able safely to abort the takeoff. Curtis W. Fitts, the captain of the doomed Electra, had not been so fortunate; he had struck the birds "at that critical instant after takeoff when the plane had ceased being a land vehicle and was not yet a controllable flying machine," in the words of William A. Leonard, a CBS News correspondent.

Twenty-six seconds after Captain Fitts had called "375 rolling" and six seconds after liftoff—at an altitude of fifty-six feet—a phalanx of starlings, spaced one per cubic foot, struck the Electra and set in motion the cascading events that killed an airliner in a little over twenty seconds. Doing what starlings do, actions written in their DNA by evolution, the Logan birds became George Murphy's "Birds of Death."

As Dr. William Drury, an ornithologist with the Massachusetts Audubon Society, suggested at the CAB hearings, the flock of starlings was probably "clumping" at the birds' impact with the Electra. Clumping is an instinctive reaction to prevent a predator from singling out one bird, which is what a peregrine falcon—the fastest creature on earth, three times faster than a cheetah—does when it plummets close to 200 miles per hour to pick off a lone starling for lunch. Starlings usually fly in a strung out pattern, but when frightened, they clump into a mass, dense and deep.

At the hearings Captain Jenkins was asked: "Now Captain, with the sudden impact of the birds on the windshield, do you feel there was a period of distraction, a period of momentary hesitation, before you made the decision to abort?" Jenkins—who looked like Audie Murphy, the Congressional Medal of Honor winner who became an actor—reflected, then replied calmly:

> I'd be . . . remiss if I didn't say that I'd been looking for something like this to happen ever since the previous accident. We're all a little bit cautious about takeoffs and landings here at Boston—LaGuardia and Idlewild too, for that matter. Naturally, we are aware of the bird situation; we do not want to become involved in it—sometimes you do. When this actually happens, to say what the time involved is when you reach up and follow through with the abortion, I'd say it was almost one instinctive motion so far as I was concerned.

Jenkins abruptly cut off the board's line of inquiry, with its implicit questioning of another experienced pilot, now dead, who had not aborted: "I had made up my mind previously; my mind is made up today. If it becomes necessary and if we're still on the ground, we'll abort. If we're airborne, we have no choice. We have to continue. It's just that in-between stage that might give you a moment's hesitation. Fortunately with me, I was still on the ground."

But Captain Fitts "was airborne at his moment of truth," as CBS's Bill Leonard noted.

No Black Box

For CAB Arthur Neumann, the CAB's chief investigator, and his six lead investigators, it was not easy to find out what happened in the cockpit of Eastern 375 in those final frantic moments. Captain Fitts had not spoken to Logan's tower then, and the flight crew had died. In the twenty-one and a half seconds before the crash, Fitts's 23,000 hours of flying experience was directed at a single goal: keeping his plane aloft.

Even if he had tried to speak to the tower, it's not evident that his words would have been heard over the huge engine vibration, especially given the old carbon mikes in use at the time; that was also true of any words spoken by the copilot or flight engineer that the pilot's mike might have picked up. Stewardess Patricia Davies testified at the hearings that the engines were "not synchronized," the left-side engines sounding "like an egg beater where something had gotten in the way of the blades." That an unusual vibration was coming from the engines was confirmed by other survivors, including Dudley Ward, the former Navy pilot, and the other stewardess, Joan Berry, who went out of her way at the hearings to confirm that there was "a terrific amount of vibration."

But no one would know for sure if any words were spoken in the cockpit, for there was no black box on board: no flight data recorder and no voice recorder.

The idea of the black box—today painted bright orange to help searchers to locate it quickly—originated in 1954, after the de Havilland Comet jet airliner explosions over Europe, but the prototype box was not produced until 1957. Both idea and prototype came from a young Australian chemist, Dr. David Warren, who normally worked on jet fuels, but who labored away privately in his off hours on his pet project. In 1960 Australia became the first country to mandate such flight recorders on aircraft, after an unexplained crash in Queensland. But Eastern 375 carried no black box.

The CAB investigators would have to solve the mystery of the crash of Eastern 375 the old-fashioned way, using their knowledge, experience, and detective skills—and those of nearly an army of helpers across the nation. Ultimately, the CAB spent twenty-two months to determine what happened to the Electra, from its takeoff roll at 17:39 (in military time) until the white geyser shot skyward at 17:40.

The CAB proceeded in a deliberate, methodical, and thoughtful manner; the investigators behaved like a bunch of good engineers. They carefully scrutinized all instruments retrieved from the plane's cockpit (one dial's arrow frozen in place by high impact or, under ultraviolet light, an arrow's position at the instant of the crash still detectable upon another dial's face) and the condition and position of the Electra's many mechanical parts (ailerons, flaps, rudder, prop petals, and the like) when the plane struck the bay, always discounting for impact damage.

What was the condition of the power plant—the four Allison turboprop engines, in aviation nomenclature—at the end of its life? Once fetched up from the bottom of the bay, with the newly arrived crabs removed, the four engines would be broken down and examined by the CAB's power plant team and then reassembled, boxed up, and shipped off for added study to the manufacturer, the Allison Division of General Motors, in Indianapolis.

Speaking in flat, unflashy language peppered with technical argot, CAB investigators sought to solve the problem and have their findings stand the test of time and of good science. When Arthur Neumann was asked how long it would take to learn the cause of the crash, he replied, "It might be four weeks or it might be four months." Although the CAB issued interim reports, its final report of the accident's probable cause was released on July 22, 1962.

Nearly all parts of the wrecked airliner were located by a legion of divers who searched freezing water, scoured muck, and felt their way by hand through slippery eel grass. Early on, Neumann had issued a public plea that every scrap of Eastern 375 be turned over to the CAB: a tiny piece of evidence could be the missing tile in the mosaic that, when dropped into place, would reveal the probable cause. Small prizes and large prizes were brought up from the bottom of the bay; for example, a water-soaked radio log book was an item of particular interest.

Once all broken sections of the airliner had been raised from the seafloor by the Navy lighter and laid upon what looked like a funeral barge, the corpse of Eastern Flight 375 was ferried across Boston Harbor in the quiet moments of an early Saturday morning—October 8—to the seaside town of Hingham, and then transferred to a warehouse at a Navy annex there. The CAB's structures team had already put chalk markings on the floor to show where different parts of the airliner were to be set down and then worked on, far from Boston hubbub, by the appropriate CAB team. Metaphorically and physically, the investigators would try to put Humpty Dumpty together again.

Since air crash investigators often work for long stretches amid piles of rubble, they have earned the nickname of tin-kickers. But given their cerebral mission and skill set, a better moniker would be one that evoked some keen-eyed detective, like Sherlock Holmes or Hercule Poirot.

As with any investigations into a fatal air crash, the CAB would try to solve two mysteries: why had the plane crashed, and what had caused injury and death to occur?

People do not have to die when an airplane crashes, although in the public mind airplane crash seems almost synonymous with death. Ask people what percent of those involved in airplane crashes survive, and they will hopelessly underestimate. The truth is that 97 percent survive. Even in a bad airliner crash, more lives could often have been saved if the passengers had been better protected.

The CAB wanted to know if more people could have survived the Electra crash and escaped from the airliner before it sank. When the Suffolk County medical examiner turned in the official cause of death for Frederick Nino Abate, it was death by drowning. Had Freddie been better protected, might he have escaped, as others did, before the fuselage sank? No one will ever know for sure. As they studied the passenger seats in the old Navy warehouse, CAB investigators would find widespread failure of seats and seat belts, even compromises of the floor meant to hold fast to seats on impact. And where the floor held, had the seats been fixed strongly enough to it?

Why were so many service trays dented in by heads and legs of people flung forward violently, restrained only by that slim belt at the waist? Many seats appeared to have broken free and collapsed accordion-style at the front of the aircraft, with the passengers crushed to death in the pileup. In short, what could the CAB learn about how the impact injuries had occurred, so as to recommend changes that might save lives in the future? Phrased differently: what had caused those severe head gashes, heavy bleeding, and broken legs that Commander Regan had spotted as he paddled his kayak across oil-slick water at the crash site?

The crash also raised a long-standing controversy over the merits of front-facing versus rear-facing seats on airliners. Passenger seats on military transports the world over tend to face rearward, while on commercial airliners they face front. Why? Which is safer? More about that later.

CBS Reports

Bill Leonard attended all three days of the January hearings, not only as a correspondent but also as the producer of a one-hour prime-time television documentary, "The Case of the Boston Electra," that would air on February 16. The executive producer of CBS Reports was the legendary Fred W. Friendly, who had teamed with Edward R. Murrow to broadcast two of the finest TV documentaries ever made—"Senator Joseph McCarthy," which helped end witch hunts for Communists in the 1950s, and "Harvest of Shame," a probe into the shocking conditions of America's migrant workers. Now teamed with Leonard, who would later help create 60 Minutes and become president of CBS News, Friendly would again bring leading-edge journalism to television. Never before had a news show given such in-depth scrutiny to an airliner crash investigation. Friendly and Leonard were examining a crash at an apt moment, offering insight and information to travelers as the United States entered a period of explosive growth in air travel—made possible by the onset of the jet age. As Leonard said in his lead-in to "The Case of the Boston Electra": "Two generations ago a few dared fly. Later many chose to fly. Today most everyone flies."

Leonard had arrived in Boston with a film crew on the morning of October 5 and set his cameras whirring as planes took off and landed at Logan Airport, while recovery work was still going on in Winthrop Harbor, under the eyes of watching gulls. Like the CAB, Leonard wanted to know why the plane had crashed, and why had so many people died.

CAB Teams

Old hands at the process, the CAB investigators divided themselves into teams: a structures team, a power plant team, an operations team, a human factors team, and a witness team. Each was headed by a CAB official but included experts and interested parties from the airlines, the manufacturers involved, the pilots' association, the flight engineers' association, and the like, to round out the team's expertise and to ensure a full and fair inquiry.

The Air Line Pilots Association always took part in such investigations, having previously criticized the FAA and the CAB for far too often ascribing blame to a dead pilot, unable to defend himself. Even if a pilot had made an error in the final moments of an emergency, an error by another party, or a chain of errors by others, might have put the pilot in the emergency, where he was expected to rescue an aircraft unnecessarily in trouble. The pilots' association recognized that for many interested parties, the easiest way out of culpability and the attendant liability was to blame the dead pilot; then those parties could return to business as usual, even if the pilot's reputation was stained and the public still at risk. The International Association of Machinists would also later come to take part in most crash investigations, since maintenance issues often arose. That is how John Goglia— once he had grown up into a fine aviation mechanic who was also straight-talking, politically astute, and a quick study—came to be involved with National Transportation Safety Board investigations, eventually developing into one of the nation's top crash experts.

Catastrophic airliner crash investigations are high-stakes ventures.

Often many lives have been lost; there are grieving families with a right to know why a loved one had been killed; millions of dollars in liability are at risk; and an airline's or manufacturer's very existence may be in question. And, psychologically, of course, no one wishes to carry the blame for a catastrophic airliner crash. As Goglia points out, the victims of an airliner crash are not limited to those aboard the flight and their grieving loved ones. The victims include anyone whose life was touched by the flight. For example, Goglia reports, the typical outcome of an air traffic controller's involvement in a midair collision is suicide within five years of the disaster.

This is why the CAB invested such care in creating a fair and equitable process of inquiry in Boston. Each morning all the CAB teams assembled and, led by Neumann, updated one other, filling in gaps and trading information—perhaps offering a report someone had of an American Airlines Electra that had recently suffered bird ingestion, or CAB data on past bird ingestions by Electras.

The witness team, with so many hot leads to pursue, split into two groups. One group returned from Winthrop beach with a filmed interview of some boys who provided valuable details on the final movements of the Electra as it flew over Winthrop Harbor.

At a CAB official's request, one articulate boy named James, perhaps eleven or twelve years old, while standing on the beach in front of his home, slowly and carefully tipped a two-foot detailed model of an Electra, held by the official, this way and that to illustrate the plane's behavior before it plunged into the bay. James's vivid recollection included which of the four propellers were turning, and at what speed, as well as a "burst of noise," "sounding almost like an explosion"—although not an explosion—just before the airliner struck the water. James had surely heard one of the engines surging back to near full power after recovering from a temporary flameout. Recall that three of the four Electra engines were working at the moment of impact, with only the number one permanently shut down. As Bartholomew Flynn had said, the Electra "appeared to be sound when she hit the water." Until the plane fell out of the sky a couple of hundred yards from shore, it had looked to James as if it were going to pass directly over the roof of his family's beach-side home.

Nearly an Army at Work

At the peak of the investigation, a small army of people was at work for the CAB, and not only the sixty in Boston, but others across the land, had weeks of long days and sleepless nights. At Lockheed in Burbank, California, test flights were done on the Electra to recreate within the limits of air safety the circumstances faced by the flight crew—especially the sequence of engine flameouts and restarts, skidding, and banking. In Indianapolis, workers at Allison minutely examined the Electra's four engines and conducted bird ingestion tests on engines identical to the Electra's—with anesthetized starlings, grackles, and blackbirds fired by air guns in ones, twos, fours, sixes, and eights into ginned-up engines. In Dayton, Ohio, bench testing was done on the crushed petals of the propeller blades retrieved from the wrecked aircraft. At the Smithsonian Institution and the U.S. Fish and Wildlife Agency in Washington, ornithologists examined charred bird remains removed from the engines of Flight 375. At Eastern Airlines' headquarters in Miami, N-5533's maintenance records and flight history were studied. Also in Miami, the CAB conducted a clever set of tests, using a new, high-fidelity Electra simulator owned by National Airlines, whose interior was a complete replica of the cockpit of the L-188.

"Don't Look for Zebras"

It is important to remember that the first theory of what caused the Electra to crash was not in fact bird ingestion. The CAB was following the prudent dictum of medical diagnosticians: "When you hear hoof beats, don't look for zebras." Or starlings. You check for the obvious first.

Given the airliner's bizarre behavior on takeoff while in the hands of a highly experienced pilot, it appeared the Electra had lost engine power soon after takeoff, especially on the left side. The signs were the sudden, flat turn to the left; the banking to the left and the skidding to the left; the couple of times when the plane bravely seemed to recover course and climb, followed by its sad sinking to half its altitude; the left wing's "falling off" (dropping) from an apparent stall (insufficient lift to hold it up), as the plane half-rolled to the left and plunged almost vertically toward the bay, spiraling into the water.

Given that crash profile, the first theory of what caused the accident was engine failure on takeoff. The only problem was that "it was not a theory that made much sense," as Robert Serling wrote in his 1963 *The Electra Story: The Dramatic History of Aviation's Most Controversial Airliner*. Serling was then aviation editor at United Press International. He is the equally gifted brother of Rod Serling, creator of television's famed *Twilight Zone*. While Rod died at the age of fifty, Robert went on to write several dozen fiction and nonfiction books, often rooted in aviation; now ninety, he is still publishing books.

The Electra, as Serling notes, was a pilot's dream in reserve power; no other airliner had so much built into it. With only two engines operating, the plane could still carve its way into the skies at 250 feet a minute. That meant in the crash at Boston "at least three and perhaps all four engines would had to have failed," and Serling noted the mathematical probability of that, conservatively estimated, was one in ten billion.

Another early theory was contaminated fuel supply, but that idea was easily ruled out. Explosives—always a media favorite—were also quickly eliminated. Within two weeks, the so-called human factor was scratched, too, including a pilot's heart attack on takeoff. The flight crew had blue-chip credentials, superb flying records, enviable experience, and up-to-date and spot-on health and flight checks.

When the Boston crash occurred, the public's mind of course flashed back to the Electra's structural problem—the one that had caused the so-called mirror image crashes at Buffalo, Texas, and Tell City, Indiana, where a wing (the left wing in the first crash and the right wing in the second crash) had surreally torn away in midflight and at high subsonic speed. Engineers from Lockheed and the National Aeronautics and Space Administration engineers finally diagnosed that problem as "whirl mode flutter." The engine mounts, once weakened or perhaps failing after a hard landing, were allowing too much gyroscopic rotational movement of the propellers at a particular frequency. As bad luck would have it, the gyroscopic propeller movement happened at the wing's natural resonance frequency, so that the gyroscopic movement was being swiftly transferred to the wing, which then began to flutter, more and more rapidly, until in half a minute the wing tore free from the aircraft.

Interestingly, in the Boston Electra crash, when the left wing lost lift and stalled, just before the plane's plunge, one aeronautical expert said it was "like losing a wing."

Through a massive modification program, Lockheed was correcting the whirl mode flutter on the entire fleet of 165 Electras. Engine mounts were redesigned and the wing dramatically stiffened; with those changes, any potential for wing flutter was eliminated. The Electras were brought to Burbank, where, production-line style, each was modified in twenty days and put back into service. But until the problem was fixed on all aircraft, the FAA set the speed limit for the Electras at 259 miles per hour, even though the plane had been designed to fly at 450. On December 30, 1960, the FAA recertified the plane to fly at its original design speed. In any case, the Boston Electra would never have flown faster than 259 miles per hour on its short hops to Philadelphia and points south. Partly for that reason, within two weeks of starting its investigation, the CAB had ruled out structural problems as the cause of the Boston crash.

That meant that the CAB was coming closer and closer to a hunt for zebras. "The Case of the Boston Electra" was taking on the quality of an Agatha Christie mystery; the solution was moving inexorably toward the improbable.

The Bird Strike Theory

By early light on October 5, rumors of bird ingestion were rife at Logan Airport. The dawn had illuminated the runways, and the airport's supervisors and technical staff noticed a large number of badly mauled bird carcasses lying to the left of Runway 9, near its intersection with Runway 15.

Today, the field of landscape ecology studies the rich biodiversity often found where one homogeneous patch of landscape borders another, differently homogeneous patch: the border between the two can be a busy place, full of interactions between ecosystems. The writer Cliff Hauptman, in his book *Finding Fish*, directs the eager fisherman to "edges," places where water meets shore or sun meets shade, as locations that fish frequent, hoping to snag something delectable to eat. Life on earth spills over from one nifty ecological niche into another—an insect happily living in East Boston marsh grass somehow ends up in the stomach of a fish; starlings dine by the shore on insects and seeds, splash themselves clean in the conveniently located water, and head to the girders of the Tobin Bridge for a good night's rest, but end up in an Electra's jet engines on takeoff, or in tatters along a runway. The edges of our living world are fascinating, sometimes dangerous places, which may be the origin of the saying, "Live life at the edge."

It is hard to imagine a place with more biodiversity than mud flats, where ocean meets shore at low tide. On October 4, 1960, that biodiversity included ancient and modern fliers in a mutually murderous collision that neither intended. Since the common term for such an event is bird strike— as in the title of this book— it is important to set the record straight out of decent regard for the birds. "Bird strike" suggests that the starlings struck the Electra. But since the Electra was flying at 151 miles per hour and the starlings were probably going at 43 miles per hour, their mean liftoff speed, the Electra was traveling three and a half times as fast as the birds. Hence, it can be more properly said the Electra struck the birds. The event was a "plane strike" on the birds. Starlings are not known to be suicidal: if the plane had been flying more slowly, they would have gotten out of its way.

It is strange that few eyewitnesses to the crash mentioned anything about birds. It appears that only Bartholomew Flynn at Deer Island, mindful of his sick dog, and one rescued passenger reported seeing birds. One other survivor recalled a "dark smudge" passing through the propellers and over the right wing, but made no mention of birds. The photos of the plane taken by Myron Williams, standing on the airfield, showed no birds. Nor did the air traffic controller mention birds. Granted, he had glanced away fleetingly from Runway 9 to glimpse the two Sabre Jets taking off, but he had watched the early portion of the Electra's takeoff roll, down to the intersection with Runway 15.

If a black cloud of 10,000 to 20,000 starlings really struck the Electra six seconds after takeoff, how could most eyewitnesses have missed it?

The answer lies in Captain Jenkins's testimony: starlings in flight are visible and invisible—the quicksilver of avian life, especially insofar as pilots are concerned. "A lazy seagull, you can pick up a wing and fly over it," Jenkins observed. "With these starlings you can't avoid them. They're zip, zip, right in front of the airplane."

One thing was sure: everything about the crash of the Boston Electra happened with frightening swiftness. Twenty seconds after ingesting birds, a modern airliner lay dead in the water, broken into two parts.

In considering the sudden mortal wound inflicted by a flock of starlings that then vanishes, with few people having seen them, one recalls a once-popular mystery set at a dinner party: no murder weapon can be found anywhere, until someone discovers an icicle was used to fatally stab the victim, only to melt and vanish into thin air. The starlings disappeared at dusk on October 4; there was no trace left of them until the dawn lit Runway 9 on October 5, revealing a brigade of dead birds. Despite the discovery of the bird carcasses, few people believed the bird strike theory at first. Why would they? The first aviation death caused by bird strike had happened long before, in 1912, when Calbraith P. "Cal" Rodgers, the first person to fly across the United States (an especially remarkable achievement for a man deaf in one ear and with reduced hearing in the other, the consequence of childhood scarlet fever) crashed and died in the surf at Long Beach, California, after a gull jammed his flight controls. But no nearly fully loaded, modern commercial airliner had ever been knocked down from the sky by mere birds—let alone by birds that weighed less than three ounces each. Could birds kill more than sixty people in less than a minute? It was a hard concept for the mind to wrap around—unless it was the quick, decisive mind of the feisty FAA chief, Elwood R. "Pete" Quesada.

As soon as the bird ingestion theory emerged, it became part of an ongoing interagency squabble between the FAA and the CAB, specifically about the Electras.

The FAA had been created in 1958 with the coming of jet passenger travel and after a series of horrific midair collisions, including one in 1956 when 128 people died over the Grand Canyon. At the time, the Grand Canyon midair collision was the worst aviation disaster in U.S. history, and it had happened over hallowed ground. The crash led to sweeping change. Safety regulation was moved from the CAB to a powerful new agency, the Federal Aviation Administration, and the FAA was given sole responsibility for determining a plane's airworthiness, establishing a single common air navigation system, and air traffic control. The CAB was left only with conducting accident investigations and making recommendations for needed improvements to the FAA and the airlines industry. But it had no power of enforcement; the CAB had lost its teeth.

Quesada, the FAA's first administrator, was a former Air Force general and President Eisenhower's personal aviation advisor. The relationship between the two men dated to World War II. Quesada was outspoken and in no way carried himself like a typical Washington bureaucrat. While CAB investigators were quiet, thoughtful, and methodical, Quesada's temperament was that of the "hot fighter pilot," as Serling wrote, noting that "fighter pilots by instinct, training, and philosophy are lone wolves."

Quesada was quick and instinctive. Also colorful, controversial, abrasive, and autocratic, he was not afraid to step on toes. He had risen rapidly through the Air Force's ranks, serving as commander of the Ninth Air Force. During World War II, he had antagonized the Pentagon by, as officers there thought, putting in jeopardy the life of a top U.S. military leader when he gave General Eisenhower his first ride in a fighter plane. The act endeared Quesada to Eisenhower and contributed to the president's appointing him the first administrator of the FAA, a post he held until Kennedy and the Democrats came to power.

Enforcement of civil air regulations "had grown slack under the politically harassed, money-starved Civil Aeronautics Authority," the FAA's predecessor agency, Serling observes. So Quesada, given "a clean broom and almost unlimited authority," proceeded "to use the broom not only for cleaning but spanking purposes." He saw himself as a reformer and arrogated to himself and his powerful new agency sole judgment of right and wrong as it applied to air travel safety. He believed his first duty was to the public—not to the aviation industry, Congress, or other federal agencies. That was not an attitude that would ingratiate him in Washington. Quesada was courageous, impatient, a maverick, and unorthodox. And worse still, as Serling asserts, "he was more often than not right."

At the time of the Boston Electra crash, Quesada had been under heavy fire for months, especially from Congress, for permitting the Electra to fly after four crashes in rapid succession. The Boston crash would be the fifth in twenty months.

The first Electra crash took place on February 3, 1959, just twenty-two days after the airliner's introduction—by Eastern Airlines—into passenger service. An American Airlines Electra from Chicago on approach to New York crashed into the East River, killing sixty-five of the seventy-two people on board. The crash was so bad that it pushed off front pages the deaths in another air crash of three of the greatest rock and roll stars of the 1950s: Buddy Holly, Jiles Perry Richardson Jr. (known as the Big Bopper), and Ritchie Valens. Their chartered plane had crashed in Clear Lake, Iowa, after takeoff on a wintry midnight, also on February 3; their deaths were forever memorialized in Don McLean's "The Day the Music Died."

Before the Electra crash into the East River, there had never been such a brief interval between an airliner's introduction and its first major crash: three weeks. While the Electra was exculpated and the crash attributed to pilot error, the two crashes in which a wing tore away—on September 29, 1959, in Buffalo, Texas, and on March 17, 1960, in Tell City, Indiana—leaving so many dead, led to the CAB's tactfully secret recommendation to the FAA that it temporarily ground the Electra until the problem was identified and fixed.

Brashly, Quesada allowed the Electras to continue to fly—but, as already mentioned, he limited the plane's speed until the wing problem was fully diagnosed and rectified. Grounding the Electra could have dealt a fatal commercial blow to the plane, as had happened to the British de Havilland Comet—which, after being temporarily grounded until its problem was fixed, never won back the public's confidence. Still, aviation history showed instances of commercial success after temporary groundings. But Quesada saw no reason to ground the Electra. Reducing its top airspeed to 259 miles per hour would reduce the stress on the wing by 50 percent or so, he calculated, and that would certainly make the airliner safe to fly. Ultimately, he was proved correct: the wing problem never happened again, either before the problem was fixed or after, when the FAA had removed its temporary limit on the plane's speed.

Commercially, slowing down the Electra would hurt enough; among the airplane's top features was high subsonic speed, far faster than that of piston-driven airliners. If the FAA limited the Electra's speed to that of other planes, why would air travelers fly the Electra? Better to board a piston-driven airliner with its time-tested safety record.

With Quesada under heavy fire for failure to ground the Electra after the mirror image crashes, an Electra inbound from Boston crashed at LaGuardia, on September 14, 1960, after hitting an eight-foot dike: it flipped over and caught fire, although all seventy-six aboard walked away from the crash—a tribute to the sturdiness of the fuselage. But few took note that the Electra was not at fault or of the durability of its structure: the common view was that another Electra that had gone down in the aircraft's short lifetime, and sick jokes abounded. Serling recorded some of these:

"Did you hear about the guy who said to the ticket agent, 'I'd like a ticket on the next Electra flight to New York'? And the agent replied, 'We don't sell Electra tickets, we sell chances.'"

"Have you joined the Electra 'Crash of the Month' yet?"

"Don't miss the new aviation play, 'Mourning Becomes the Electra.'"

"Have you read the new Electra book, *Look Ma, No Wings?*"

Now, against the backdrop of this furor, in the early evening of October 4, the FAA chief was returning home from an arduous trip to the Soviet Union to study that country's aviation system. As Quesada's taxi came to a stop outside of his home in Washington, his wife raced into the street and said, "Pete, there's been a bad Electra crash." Quesada's reaction, captured by Serling, was, "Well, I'll be damned." The crash had occurred only minutes earlier.

On hearing the Electra crashed on takeoff, Quesada felt a measure of relief, since it suggested that the cause of the crash was not wing flutter. Still, he knew he would be attacked, especially in Congress. After the Boston crash, Senator Vance Hartke of Indiana, the state where the Tell City disaster occurred, said, as Serling notes: "the blood will be on Quesada's hands if one more goes down."

"Pete, Do You Know about the Dead Birds?"
What Quesada would do after the crash of the Boston Electra would parallel his actions after the mirror image crashes. Then he had decided to go it alone, although 162 people had died in Electra crashes since the plane joined the U.S. fleet of commercial airliners in January 1959.

Soon after Quesada decided to disregard the CAB's secretly submitted CAB recommendation that the FAA temporarily ground the Electra, the recommendation became public—the source probably someone at the CAB. Had the FAA chief chosen the easier path and temporarily grounded the Electra, he would have had the support of Congress and the CAB. However, Quesada was ultimately proven correct: the Lockheed Electra L-188s went on to lead long, productive lives worldwide, with some still in flight today.

As John Goglia has observed, the second and third generations of an aircraft are often safer, with early shortcomings put right. Potential shortcomings in aircraft design can be identified earlier today through the use of computer-aided design technologies. With such modern tools, somebody might have noticed that the L-188's design, in Serling's words, had taken the "conventional, straight wings into speed areas not far away from those of the forthcoming pure jets with their swept-back wings, which were designed to absorb subsonic turbulence." While that pushing of conventional straight-wing design into risky areas might have played a part in the mirror image crashes, it had nothing at all to do with the Boston Electra crash. That crash was all about a fateful encounter between ancient and modern fliers.

Quesada flew into Boston at 6:00 a.m. on the morning of October 5. As he was getting into a car to take him to a CAB briefing, he was flagged down by a Logan official, actually one he did not particularly cotton to. The man shouted, "Pete, do you know about the dead birds?" Although he hesitated, Quesada's curiosity got the better of him, and he sped off with the airport official to see the bird carcasses next to Runway 9. Quesada could see that there were many dead birds, spread broadly across an area some 200 by 800 feet to the left of the runway. Quesada had someone do quick calculations of Eastern 375's weight at takeoff. They decided that all those dead birds lay just about where the Electra would have broken from the runway.

Quesada immediately asked a Harvard ornithologist, Dr. Raymond Paynter, to examine samples of the bird remains on the runway; he did and identified the birds as starlings. Paynter offered the additional information that flocks of starlings could contain tens of thousands of birds.

"I Communed with Myself"

"I knew people would laugh at me if I said birds could knock down an Electra. But I communed with myself and decided to announce that the Electra crash was caused by impact with thousands of starlings and that the massive ingestion resulted in multiple engine failure," Quesada told Serling in an interview after the FAA chief's retirement.

As it turned out, Quesada was right on all the essentials—although wrong about quantities. There were not, as he publicly asserted a couple of days after the crash, 60,000 to 84,000 starlings in the flock that struck the Electra on takeoff. The CAB found no witnesses that testified to seeing such a huge flock. Nor did the CAB find "hundreds" of dead birds to the left of the takeoff runway, as Quesada announced— rather, investigators found seventy-five to a hundred birds, with thirty having been dead for a couple of weeks. But why had those thirty died? Had their deaths gone unnoticed as harbingers of the disaster to come? Had the starlings struck an aircraft, not fatefully straight into the jet turbine engines, but elsewhere, perhaps at the wings or against the fuselage?

Paynter reported that the birds on the runway had been killed in the daytime, since he had found seeds and insects in their stomachs, which meant they had been killed shortly after eating. In the starling, as with all birds, food passes through the body quickly, within the hour.

Quesada's "battlefield solution" to the mystery of the crash would prove quite close to the truth; it is hard to find anything but quantities to quibble about between what he said and what the CAB stated in its final report, twenty-two months later. Quesada told Serling: "I knew a single bird had been known to cause a temporary flame-out (failure) in a turbine engine, so I thought to myself that impact with and subsequent ingestion of a flock of birds was a reasonable and logical explanation for what happened."

When Quesada announced his conclusions a couple of days after the crash, he added that "a turbine engine will quit if anything disturbs the delicate balance between the mixture of air with fuel." Right after that statement, the CAB's Arthur Neumann was quoted in *The Boston Globe*, obviously distancing himself from Quesada's swift diagnosis: "It seems highly unlikely that the birds could get by the propellers and into the intake—particularly in such a short period of time. But we are not discounting anything. Until we get the wreck up where we can inspect it, we can't say much."

Quesada was wholly impolitic to say anything about the crash so early; he should have prudently deferred to the CAB investigation that had barely begun. Still, Neumann's comment backfired. In the same article with Neumann's remarks, a jet engine expert stated: "Small birds in quantity are more dangerous than the larger birds because the larger type deflect more easily. Moreover, a great flock of birds coming in contact with an airliner's engines at a distinct angle of flight can be extremely dangerous."

Neumann's observation that propeller blades would be a barrier to bird entry into jet engines was also undermined by another jet engine expert, who offered a compelling image: "If one threw a snowball at the air intake through the propellers whirling at 1200 r.p.m, it would get through nine times out of ten."

A Quiet Pursuit of the Scientific

Once Pete Quesada pronounced the cause of the crash to be bird strike—despite his caveat that this was just his casual opinion and was subject to change in the face of dominating evidence to the contrary—in the public's mind, federal authorities had diagnosed the cause of the crash. It was hardly the public's job to decode the alphabet soup of government agencies—what the CAB takes care of, and what the FAA takes care of. Quesada had stepped outside the bounds of the FAA and squarely onto the toes of the CAB.

The CAB's mandate was not to make a heuristic leap to a solution, even if it was the correct one. In contrast, that is exactly what a "hot fighter pilot" needs to do to in a fast-moving dogfight. So careful was the CAB that even in final reports it only issued statements of probable cause. What seemed so firmly cause at one moment might prove not to be later, given new information provided by science, engineering, weather, and the like. In the here and now, all that can be known is probable cause.

The CAB's investigation had barely gotten underway when Quesada pronounced what had caused the Boston crash. The CAB was irked by his intrusion, another issue to be dealt with. In the early stages of any investigation, the CAB was often swatting away cockamamie ideas. With nothing as yet proved or disproved, everyone felt entitled to offer up pet theories. In the Boston crash, for example, someone suggested that jet turboprop engines sound like crickets, and that the flock of starlings had rammed themselves into the jet engines in pursuit of the insects. And a newspaper reporter with no aeronautical qualifications proposed that the air intake area of jet engines be screened, and large automobile-like windshield wipers be rigged to wipe away crushed birds from the screens. But unlike a soft summer rain falling upon on automobile windshield, bird strikes can be a swift hammering, a massive assault. And jet engines require vast air intake; any blocking of air flow can cause the engine to quit, even if the blocking is caused by a screen, crushed bird remains, and a swishing wiper. What's more, as Goglia has noted, it is possible for the screen itself to be sucked into a powerful jet engine. A screen could be more of a problem than birds, "which are easier for the engine blades to chop up and pass through."

Now, in addition to such commonly tossed up theories and ideas, offered by amateurs, the CAB had to deal with the FAA chief's early public entry into an investigation that was clearly the CAB's responsibility. Also, given the continuing fracas between Congress and Quesada over the Electra, the House subcommittee on aviation decided to come up to Boston on October 10 for "their own look-see and private hearing," as Leonard described it—with CAB officials having to serve as the Congressmen's personal guides, taking them by way of "a covey of helicopters" from Logan to Hingham to tour the wreckage. To Quesada's relief, the Congressmen left Boston after two days of briefings, feeling that the Electra's structural problem appeared to have had nothing to do with the crash at Logan.

Given eyewitnesses who had seen smoke or fire emitted from the engines and the bird remains found in the engines—and with the FAA chief's imprudent pronouncement of bird strike as cause—the CAB wanted Allison engineers to scrutinize the engines. They also wanted new bird ingestion tests done on working, hot-fired engines identical to those on the Electra. Neumann went to Indiana himself to observe the testing, and Bill Leonard went along, with his cameras.

After checking the engines brought out of Winthrop harbor, Allison engineers determined all the engines to be structurally sound—free of damage, except for that caused by impact. They also found that the engines were probably producing nearly full takeoff power when the Electra crashed, except for the number one engine, which had permanently shut down. Allison engineers then fired those unlucky anesthetized starlings and starling-sized birds, each weighing two to four ounces, into fired-up engines identical to the engines on the Electra. The engineers did so using varying numbers of birds in various sequences, and dutifully recorded ingestion events with high-speed stroboscopic photography—which snapped 6,000 images per second—along with coordinated snapshots of instrument reactions and exhaust reaction. The more birds ingested, the more violent was the exhaust reaction. CBS Reports showed a film of the ingestions in its documentary; for most viewers, it was the first time they had seen the miracle of such photography, which captured the events as birds were shredded by fast-spinning turbine blades and sudden loud bursts of torchlight emanated from the rear of the jet engines. That was probably the light that Mrs. Abate saw as she watched the Electra from Logan's observation deck.

At the public CAB hearings, an Allison representative described the company's tests, eager to get on the official record two points in particular: that they "never encountered flameout at any time even with ingestion of eight birds," and that during the tests, "the engines either recovered quickly or remained in a condition that would burn the turbine blades in a few seconds. There was never a prolonged loss of power and recovery." But the CAB also had the benefit of other bird ingestion tests done by Lockheed and the FAA in Burbank, even using the Lockheed wind tunnel. Even those tests, however, still lacked the in-flight response to bird ingestion. Flying airplanes is not like a bench-tested experiment. Ask any pilot: it's as real as real can be.

The CAB would determine that prolonged loss of power was not the issue in this crash. The temporary loss of engine power on take-off, when the plane was at its most vulnerable and at a low altitude— suffered across several engines—proved fatal to the Electra, particularly with engines failing and recovering unpredictably. On earth, if you are a bird or an airplane, taking off is the hardest thing you can do. If something goes wrong, it often has a bad outcome. And the CAB stated in its final report that flameouts did occur with engine testing when enough birds were ingested. The CAB's judgment was based on the Allison and Lockheed engine testing taken together, plus, investigators' real-life perception of what happened to Eastern 375. The engine examination and testing also proved that Bartholomew Flynn's odd comment—"she appeared to be sound when she hit the water"—was brilliantly correct. All four engines were found to be structurally sound at impact, with three of four operating at nearly full takeoff power. Had God reached out a massive hand the instant before the crash, grabbed the aircraft, and set it high aloft in Magee's "delirious burning blue" with three functioning engines, the Electra could probably have resumed its flight to Philadelphia.

Sixteen Pilots

In 1961, the CAB invited sixteen top airline captains, the highest-rated Electra pilots in the United States from the thousand or so certified to fly the plane, to Miami, where National Airlines maintained its fabulous new Electra simulator—today the machine would be worth eight million dollars—known to be the most accurate electronic reproduction of an Electra in existence. Other than being asked to climb into the left seat and take off, the pilots were told nothing.

The CAB had programmed the simulator on takeoff to present the pilots with the probable sequence of events in Boston.

- Impact with birds twenty-six seconds after takeoff roll begins, and six seconds after liftoff—at an altitude of fifty-six feet. Birds ingested in one second.
- Number one engine suffers total power loss.
- Number two engine loses power for five to eight seconds, then surges back to nearly full power.
- Number three engine falters for a second or two, just a heartbeat but long enough to cause an electric power failure—and hence the hydraulic boost fails, meaning loss of power steering by the pilot. Abruptly the power steering comes back on, after the pilot has manually overcompensated.
- Number four engine loses power for four to six seconds.

All sixteen top-rated airline captains crashed. Also trying his hand at the controls was Najeeb E. Halaby, who had just replaced Pete Quesada as the new FAA chief. Halaby was a skilled pilot and a former test pilot. (He later became more famous as the father of Queen Noor of Jordan, the former Lisa Najeeb Halaby.)

The pilots were told to try again. This time the CAB fed into the simulator all the same accident factors, except one: this time number three engine kept full power, since it was never proved that that engine had shut down—which meant no electrical failure and no hydraulic boost shutdown, with attendant loss of power steering. Stewardess Joan Berry, who had miraculously escaped from the crash almost uninjured and was alert on impact, reported that the airplane's lights never went off.

But the change in programmed events did not make much difference; on the second attempt, all but a few of the pilots crashed again. And as Serling recalls, "All were somewhat shaken by the experience, emerging from the simulator with their shirts sweat-stained."

The CAB conducted sixty-six such mock flights in the simulator. "Once the guinea-pig pilots knew what to expect, they did better," Serling notes. "Captain Charles Ruby of National, for example, crashed the first time, but on his next nine make-believe take-offs he got away safely on five." With both advance warning and prior experience, the best-performing pilot of, in effect, a thousand certified Electra pilots still cracked up his airliner 44 percent of the time. Not a statistic to warm the hearts of air travelers. Realizing the limitations of tests on a trainer, the CAB believed that the results showed that simulating the conditions "prevailing at Boston demonstrated that control of the aircraft, under such conditions, could have been an insurmountable task."

No Advance Warning

Captain Fitts of course had no advance warning and no prior experience. Here is what the CAB believed confronted Fitts after he struck the flock of starlings. Of course none of the engine tests, nor the new flight tests done by Lockheed, could produce the fluctuating engine power conditions confronted by Fitts during the twenty and a half seconds he was airborne following the bird ingestion and before his plane struck the bay, all the while probably unable to see anything out of the cockpit and with no reliable airspeed readout. For three of those seconds, he was in an uncontrolled nose dive into Winthrop Harbor.

Number one engine: At least four birds ingested; propeller autofeathers. (The Electra was armed with a feature that automatically caused the propeller to "feather" if an engine's power decayed to the point where it was not contributing to thrust. Feathering adjusts the propeller pitch, so that the blades face into the airstream, edge on, to reduce drag. Autofeathering of one propeller disarmed the feature on all remaining propeller systems, the reason why no other propellers on the Boston Electra autofeathered.) When the number one autofeathers, the captain correctly shuts the engine down.

Number two engine: Six birds ingested; the most adversely affected engine, excluding the autofeathering of the number one. The number two engine flames out; a torching relight ensues with flames and a loud burst of noise emitted from the tailpipe; the engine recovers substantial power, but for critical seconds produces less than half its expected power. With the number one shut down and the number two dysfunctional, there is substantial power asymmetry, with most power on the right side. The plane is skidding, banking, yawing to the left, toward Winthrop Harbor and its horrible destiny.

Number three engine: Only one gull feather found in the cooling duct to the generator; hence, probably no bird ingestion, no loss of engine power, and no loss of power steering.

Number four engine: Probably fewer birds ingested than in numbers one and two.

In its final report, the CAB concluded that "the key to the severity and probably to the occurrence of the accident lies in the unique and critical sequence of a rapidly occurring set of events." The recovery of the number two engine "could not arrest the rapid decrease in speed before the aircraft stalled." While the relighting of the number two engine reduced the degree of power asymmetry, it could not compensate for the high-power condition on the right side. Yawing and rolling to the left were still happening, with accompanying greater and greater drag—which could only be overcome with more and more thrust, and that was unavailable because of the overall power loss. In addition, the pilot could not tell what was going on since his airspeed indicators had probably failed or were not reliable. Cascading events had overtaken the aircraft. The only recovery from the situation prior to stall and spin into the bay would have been for the pilot to cut power and lower the nose to regain control and airspeed—but given the extremely low altitude, somewhere around 100 to 150 feet, such a recovery was impossible.

"We Realized We Were Going Down"

At the CAB's public hearing, everything hung on the testimony of those who had actually been inside the aircraft when it crashed into Winthrop Harbor. Why wouldn't they be the stars? After all, only ten of seventy-two people on board had survived. While nine of the ten survivors were interviewed by the CAB, the CBS Reports documentary included filmed testimony of three—probably chosen because their aviation backgrounds gave them credibility: Dudley Ward, the former Navy pilot, and Joan Berry and Patricia Davies, the stewardesses.

Here, first is Dudley Ward, who was interviewed and filmed in his hospital bed, where he was recovering from injuries: "I do remember eventually we got to the end of the runway and started down. My first recollection that something wasn't quite right was a noise I heard from the left-hand engines. I am having a little difficulty in identifying what was normal and what was abnormal, but there was a different sound."

Ward was then asked if he recalled the aircraft's leaving the runway's surface—its liftoff. He affirmed that he did. "Did you sense anything wrong or do you recall anything being wrong, prior to this time?" the investigator asked. "Yes, I think so," Ward replied. "The plane wasn't going down the runway smoothly and straight, the way it normally would. It was weaving around somewhat." He added: "As it broke from the runway, it took a sharp turn to the left, a very sudden and very violent one; and I remember reaching for my seat belt and tightening it up. It was from that point on that everything went blank."

Dudley Ward was apparently the only eyewitness, either on the airplane or on the ground, who reported that the plane had been weaving during the takeoff roll. Joan Berry had testified: "It was just an ordinary takeoff, going down the runway. It was only after we had gained some altitude that you could tell there was something wrong. But everything was just according to procedure at first."

If Ward's observation were correct, it could suggest that Captain Fitts had seen the flock of starlings while on the ground and took some evasive action. But Berry's testimony contradicted Ward's. The CAB took no notice of Ward's comment in their final report or on the detailed map that accompanied the report. The map includes a dark line tracking the progress of Eastern 375 from its initial takeoff roll to the crash, giving no indication of untoward movement or noteworthy events during the takeoff roll—although it clearly marks the plane's veering after liftoff and annotates the map with important events that occurred at the point of bird strike and after, including the crash into the bay. In fact, the map has a dark arrow pointing straight at the takeoff roll with the CAB's comment: "Take off roll normal." Given that Berry, who flew regularly in the aircraft, reported all had been routine until the aircraft was airborne, that no other witnesses reporting weaving on the runway, and that Ward himself reported that he was not paying much attention to what was going on around him— absorbed as he was in reading the evening newspaper—it is possible that Ward, though he was a former Navy pilot, mistook the plane's low, slow climb after liftoff as its not having broken from the runway. While there was definitely veering before the "sudden, violent turn to the left" that caused Ward to tighten his seatbelt, that appears to have occurred only after liftoff from Runway 9.

Had the CAB found credible evidence of the pilot's seeing the flock of birds while on the ground and taking evasive measures to avoid the flock, the board would surely have included that in its final report.

In their testimonies, Joan Berry and Patricia Davies confirmed a reduction in power, followed by a sudden burst of power—which is consistent with an engine's temporary loss of power after bird ingestion and its coming back to power, after it had chewed up the birds in its turbine blades and relit the engine, as happened with engine number two. Berry said: "There was a sudden burst of power after we got in trouble. . . . The engines didn't sound normal at all." The reduction in power before a sudden burst of power probably happened twice. Davies clearly recalled one sudden burst of power, and then she added that she believed there was a second, which occurred just before she blacked out; she regained consciousness only after the plane was in the water. The second burst of power is probably what young James heard from the beach at Winthrop just before the plane hit the water.

As Berry was concluding her testimony, one investigator asked, "Prior to impact, did you know of an impending accident?" She coolly replied: "Yes, we realized we were going down."

The CAB Chief Finally Speaks

On February 16, 1961, the day the CAB released its interim report, Alan Boyd, the new CAB chief, was interviewed on camera by Bill Leonard. With the CAB report and the filmed interview of Boyd in hand, Fred Friendly decided to air "The Case of the Boston Electra" that night. The documentary would be seen by millions, for CBS News was then the most respected national television news outlet, its journalists known to have been shaped by the high standards set by Edward R. Murrow.

In the interview, Boyd stated that the accident clearly would not have occurred if the airplane had not struck a flock of birds immediately after takeoff: "Our report shows that the airplane was functioning properly at the time it started down the runway and when it got into the air. The plane then ran into a flock of birds—how many we don't know, but apparently a substantial number." Some birds were ingested into the Electra's turboprop engines, Boyd confirmed. The plane was in the air about twenty-seven seconds. From the time the plane struck the birds and suffered power loss, the crew had "maybe five seconds to decide what was wrong, analyze the situation, see what they could do, and then do it. After that very limited time there was nothing anybody could do. In aviation parlance the crew became passengers."

Boyd emphasized that the CAB "doesn't believe it's possible to train a crew of human beings to react to such a situation as this crew was faced with, within the limited amount of time available." Leonard then asked: "So would that put the accident in the unavoidable category?" Boyd replied carefully:

> I don't think you could say it was in the unavoidable category. I think that, if the crew of that plane was blessed with an instinct, which certainly would have been a gift of God under the circumstances, to do immediately exactly the right thing, they might have been able to succeed in having a controlled crash. But the plane was going to crash after they hit the birds: there's no question in our minds about that.

Boyd never specified what the crew might have done if inspired by that special instinct that would have been a gift of God. Clearly, since the plane was going to crash anyhow, all Captain Fitts might have done was to set the plane down instantly, after the plane had suffered power losses. But he had no maneuvering room: the strike occurred at fifty-six feet of altitude, and his control of the aircraft was limited by asymmetric power loss and the rapid approach of the end of the runway, with the sea and populated Winthrop beyond. Oh yes, and his windshield was probably impenetrably covered with bird remains and he did not know his airspeed.

The CAB estimates that the Electra's wheels were probably up at 12.5 seconds after liftoff, which puts Fitts already at the outer limit of Boyd's five seconds to act. The pilot would have had to order wheels down and hope they were down, locked in place, when his plane touched back down. Belly landings on the ground are not the best way to try to save an airliner loaded with 25,000 pounds of jet fuel with a flashpoint of 100 degrees Fahrenheit. Would the landing gear have descended in time? Not likely.

Since the plane was veering sharply leftward after the bird strike, it is also not likely that the pilot could have put the Electra squarely and neatly down on Runway 9, properly facing due east, especially since he probably could see nothing out the windshield. The primary advantage to a controlled crash landing would have been that the plane would have been moving horizontally, dissipating deceleration forces, and—most important—keeping the fuselage intact, which tends to save passenger lives. A horizontal controlled crash landing offers better prospects of survival than a near vertical uncontrolled crash. But, as the CAB effectively said, a controlled crash landing that day was not humanly possible. God would have had to be on the flight deck.

Lesson Learned

In the interview, Bill Leonard asked the CAB chief: "What have you learned from the crash of the Boston Electra?" Boyd answered: "Several things that I think will be of considerable importance in the future of commercial and other types of aviation; most important of all . . . the operational problems that are created by the possibility of bird ingestion in jet air intakes or turboprop air intakes." Boyd acknowledged that during the original Electra certification process, there had been a number of tests done on the turboprop engines to ascertain whether the engine would continue to operate after the ingestion of stones or birds, "but no consideration was given to the operational problems that faced a crew when they are flying the airplane when birds are ingested." He added, "Some stimulus must be given to this proposition, and design considerations have to be undertaken that hopefully will bring about a design that will eliminate the possibility of birds in any quantity being ingested into engines in the future."

Boyd made it clear that he was speaking of any jet turboprop or turbo-jet engine, since both operate the same way: "through the flow of air going in through the turbine section." Leonard then inquired, "Do you and your colleagues at the CAB fly the Electra?" Smiling, Boyd said, "Definitely. I think it's one of the best airplanes I've ever flown."

At that point, Leonard asked the CAB chief about lessons in survival gained from the investigation into the Boston crash. Boyd instantly turned to the fact that so many passenger seats had torn loose from their moorings. He was careful to say that he was not implying the seats on the Electra or any other airliner were not safe, but that the condition in which they found the seats "leads us to believe that we have not reached the ideal in safety so far as seats are concerned," and so more testing needed to be done to explore the possibility of a new design: "We are reaching into areas where we don't really know all the answers yet, and I think the facts in this accident will help fill in some of the blank pieces in the jigsaw puzzle that will lead us ultimately to the ideal seat."

Dr. Harley Davidson

In "The Case of the Boston Electra," Leonard used Boyd's comment about the need to seek an ideal seat design to introduce a segment on a long-standing controversy in the aviation industry: which are safer, seats that face the front of the plane, or those that face the rear?

The CBS Reports team had traveled to the Armed Forces Institute of Pathology at Walter Reed Hospital in Washington, which investigated the medical aspects of all major U.S. air crashes. Leonard knew that, on all regular Military Air Transport Service (MATS) flights, U.S. servicemen rode backward, as did servicemen in Great Britain, where the Royal Air Force stated resolutely: "Rear facing seats must reduce fatalities in the long run." But commercial airline passengers all around the world faced front—as they still do today. Why wasn't this debate settled? If the Boston Electra's passengers had faced rearward, would more of them have been saved—including ironically more of the fifteen marine recruits traveling to boot camp, not on a MATS flight but on a commercial airliner? Perhaps Freddie Abate would have been alive if he had been flown to Parris Island by the military and not by Eastern Airlines.

The pathologist in charge of the investigation into the Boston crash bore the unlikely name of Dr. Harley Davidson, and the rank of captain. Leonard asked him what had caused the fatalities in the Electra crash. Davidson used a dummy to show the camera how each passenger was facing forward, tied down with a small, thin seat belt. In a crash on land or on water, Davidson showed that the feet and head are violently flung forward at the same time; in the great majority of cases, that results in fractured legs and heads. He also reported that most seats on the Electra tore loose from the flooring at the back of the seat, the most logical place "because you're still tied down with the seat belt, and when the passenger goes forward, he pulls the seat with him." He demonstrated how the seat with the passenger rams into the seat in front of him: "And when they tear loose the seats are jammed together, like an accordion; they all end up in the front of the aircraft, with the passengers smashed in between." Davidson declined to speculate how many more passengers might have been saved if they had been facing the rear, although he had gone over the entire matter carefully with the CAB. It was clear that whether the floor stayed intact was also a significant factor: "If we had the proper conditions, consisting of a stronger floor, rearward facing seats, and a firmer tie-down—it's difficult to say—but I would say more."

At this juncture, the U.S. Air Force chief pathologist, Colonel Frank Townsend—highly experienced, bluff, and blunt—joined the conversation to respond to Leonard's question of what should be done about seat safety on commercial airliners. There may well be something about performing thousands of autopsies on young Americans that makes you forthright. In any case, Townsend said: "The answer is simple. Turn the seats around and stress them to the floor properly." Commercial airlines, he believed, should switch to rearward-facing seats, "stressed to the floor to 16 to 20 g's, same as the Military Air Transport System requires." The result would be that "a whole lot of people killed in accidents now would survive, or at least have a chance to get out of the aircraft and have a chance to save their lives."

In 1960, seats on commercial airliners were stressed to the floor to 9 g's—nine times the force of gravity. The push to 16 g's is something that John Goglia fought for across the decades. The 9 g's standard was set in 1952 and persisted until the FAA finally approved a 16 g's requirement, effective with aircraft built after October 2009, with the standard also applying to the flooring and the tracks the seats ride on. As a practical matter, starting in the 1990s, most planes were near 16 g's qualified.

As regards front- versus rear-facing seats, Bill Leonard and his camera crew went off to interview Irving Pinkel, who worked for NASA and had overseen the crashing of forty full-sized surplus airplanes to understand the effects of crashes on the human body. Dummies aboard the planes had been wired to send back radio signals about impact forces upon them, with rapid-fire photos snapped of the dummies as they were flung about the aircraft. The planes were crashed at different speeds and impact angles. In the interview, Pinkel's brilliance is clear as he explains the complexity of the matter of front- versus rear-facing seats. In certain crashes, rear-facing seats offer greater protection—especially if the floor to which they are affixed remains intact. But in some crashes, depending on the speed and angle of the aircraft on impact, front-facing seats can be safer. In 1960, there was no facility where seat designs could be tested, to develop that "ideal seat" of which Boyd had spoken. No one seat manufacturer could afford to build and maintain such a facility.

Pinkel also pointed to two important matters affecting seat construction. First, airplanes have weight limits, so in evaluating the ideal seat, its construction, and its stressing to the floor, it is necessary to consider that if seats become too heavy, they can endanger the overall safety of the aircraft. Second, it is impossible not to consider the comfort of the passenger; airline passengers are not astronauts or test pilots.

Incidentally, Pinkel later became a key investigator of the Apollo 1 disaster, in which three astronauts were killed by fire on the launch pad, and the Apollo 13 explosion, when a lunar-landing team was safely returned to earth against all odds: the so-called successful failure. Pinkel is also credited with giving Neil Armstrong, the first person to set foot on the moon, his first job as a test pilot. Pinkel's life's work included reducing the frequency of fires in crashes and designing airplane seats that reduce the effects of crash impact.

Probable Cause
On July 26, 1962, the CAB issued its final report on the crash of Eastern 375, which included this valediction: "The Board determines that the probable cause of this accident was the unique and critical se-

quence of the loss and recovery of engine power following bird ingestion, resulting in loss of airspeed and control during takeoff."

And the CAB added that "emergency conditions of great complexity were thrust upon the crew in an increasingly deleterious environment, and that human capabilities of perception, recognition, analysis, and reaction were insufficient in the time and space restrictions of this accident to accomplish restoration of positive performance control."

Despite the cogent, unflashy, engineer-like language, that statement has a quality of poetry about it, in its compression of language and its compassion for the limits of human capability. It recognizes our frailty and our vulnerability.

In the television series *John Adams*, there is a moment when John Adams, Abigail Adams, and Thomas Jefferson are in Paris together, witnessing the first flight of a hot-air balloon. As the tether is released and the balloon pushes skyward, Jefferson says: "So, our umbilical cord to Mother Earth has been severed for the first time in history. Mankind floats upon a limitless plane of air."

As we have seen, the cutting of that cord brought new joy and knowledge to humankind, and with it grave danger.

5 Sharing the Skies: The Problems

In the next life, let us be birds.
—Jennifer Jones to William Holden,
in *Love Is a Many-Splendored Thing*

We admire birds. We envy them. We idealize their boundless freedom as do the star-crossed lovers on a high and windy hill in
"Love Is a Many-Splendored Thing." Yet, in some deep, Jungian place
in our collective unconscious, we also fear birds for their special powers—as fully evidenced in ancient myth and modern film, with a
remake of Hitchcock's terrifying 1963 *The Birds* due for release in
2011.

As hazardous as birds are to human flight—420 planes have been
destroyed and more than 400 people have been killed by bird and other
wildlife strikes, making them the second-leading cause of aviation-
related fatalities—we should consider ourselves lucky that real birds
are not as homicidal as Hitchcock's, nor as well-armed as the ones
described below from Greek myth. The italicized excerpts are from
Jason and the Golden Fleece: The Argonautica, an epic poem by Apol-
lonius of Rhodes, translated by Richard Hunter (Oxford: Clarendon
Press of Oxford University Press, 1993).

When Jason and the Argonauts—a dream team of famed warriors—entered the Black Sea in pursuit of the Golden Fleece, a bird
from the island of Ares, where the god of war lived, flew over Jason's
ship and fired from one of its wings a metallic feather that lodged in
the body of Oileus, whose oar fell away from his hands.

The crew stared in wonder at the feathered arrow. Clever Amphidamas devised a plan. Half the crew would row toward Ares, while the other half would make a roof for the ship of overlapping bronze shields held fast by interlaced spears. As they approached Ares, Amphidamas instructed, "*Everyone together give out a mighty scream, so that the birds will take fright at the strange racket. If we reach the island itself, then make a terrible din both with your shields and yelling aloud.*" Beneath their roof, the crew could not see the birds, but *as the Argonauts drew near to the island and beat on their shields, countless thousands immediately took off in every direction in panicked flight.* And *as they flashed high up over the sea towards the mountains rising on the horizon,* the birds sent down upon the ship a volley of metallic arrows, which clattered like a winter hailstorm upon the roofs of the warriors' homes. Among the crew was the great Heracles, who had encountered these man-attacking birds before. As one of his twelve labors, he had to rid Lake Stymphalos of their menace. Carrying giant bronze rattles fashioned for him by Hephaestus, he had ascended a mountain near the lake and shaken the rattles until the birds flew off, screeching in fear.

Such an assault by arrow-shooting birds surely qualifies as a bird strike and is far more colorful than what we label a bird strike today— almost always a fast-moving aircraft's overtaking a bird or flock of birds traveling at a far slower speed. But, with the aid of a little phys-ics, we will learn later that the consequences of such a strike can be no less deadly than the type described in Greek myth.

Sharing the Skies

There are 100 billion birds on earth and 6.8 billion people—ten thou-sand species of birds, and one species of humankind. Neither bird nor human is about to stop flying; hence, when it comes to bird strikes upon aircraft, the only reasonable question is: can't we all get along? Can't we find a way of sharing the skies safely with the avian life we so longed to be like? As the only species to fly without having evolved natural wings, we are clearly the intruders in the sky. The mounting danger of lethal bird strikes upon large airliners, packed with hundreds of people, might finally be the spur to action, to our finding a way for ancient fliers and modern fliers to get along in the sky. Human flight is no longer two clever and persistent bicycle makers in the wind-swept dunes of the Outer Banks in North Carolina. Every day men, women, and children—including those we love—take wing into increasingly dangerous flyways, inhabited by a hundred billion birds; many big, traveling in flocks—some by night—that are capable of knocking out of the sky even a two-hundred-million-dollar aircraft.

For a half-century, the crash of Eastern 375 has held the record for the worst air crash caused by bird strike—even as new generations of airliners have come and gone, new airports have been built by the hundreds around the globe, and new records have been set and broken for the number of daily air travelers and the number of aircraft flights. Logan International Airport alone, now the twenty-third busiest in the world, handles 400,000 takeoffs and landings a year. The National Air Traffic Controllers Association reports that 87,000 flights are in U.S. skies every day, and every year air traffic controllers handle sixty-four million takeoffs and landings. It is a sorry comment that the clearest the earth's air had been in a long time was during the several days after 9/11, when the U.S. commercial fleet was grounded, their contrails erased from the skies.

But Eastern 375's record will not last for much longer. A confluence of factors points to an air catastrophe soon, dwarfing in loss of life those who died in the Boston Electra crash. Indeed, the same confluence of factors suggests possible successive air disasters caused by bird strike, with heavy loss of life, unless urgently needed measures are taken.

The confluence of factors was clearly manifested in one of the most uplifting news story of 2009—the miracle on the Hudson referred to in the preface of this book. On January 15, US Airways Flight 1549, an Airbus A320 flying out of LaGuardia Airport in New York to Charlotte, North Carolina, with 155 passengers and crew on board, struck a flock of Canada geese over the Bronx at 3,000 feet, ninety seconds after takeoff. The plane's two jet engines shut down, the aircraft powerless above a metropolis with twice the number of passengers on board as the Boston Electra had carried. The gifted fifty-eight-year-old pilot, Captain Chesley B. "Sully" Sullenberger, realizing he did not have sufficient altitude to glide his plane back to LaGuardia or reach another airport, instead glided his 140,000-pound airliner to a safe landing on the Hudson River. Although the ditching of an airliner usually ends in disaster, everyone on board survived, and only a few people had even minor injuries. Luckily, the emergency water landing took place on what is called flat water—calm and wave-free— and as New York City's afternoon rush hour was about to begin, with ferry boats ready to carry commuters and captains at their helms. In a flash, ferry boats reached the airliner floating on the Hudson River, its passengers gathered on the wings, some of the women in high heels. Cool and heroic, Captain Sullenberger walked the plane's aisle twice to be sure that no one remained aboard before he too stepped out of the airliner and boarded a rescue craft.

It was a thrilling, heartwarming story, especially welcome to a nation in free fall toward a major recession; a tale of what could happen in a moment of danger in the sky, with a heroic and skillful captain of vast experience at the controls, aided by a seasoned crew and Lady Luck.

The story is also an instructive one, mostly because such an event is not likely to happen again with so positive an outcome. After the next disabling bird strike above a major city, it is hard to believe there will be another uniquely qualified captain at the controls, with an equally fortunate concatenation of circumstances to follow. Rather, the news will be that an ill-fated airliner on takeoff struck a flock of very large birds and that, having lost all power, it crashed onto urban streets and slid into occupied buildings, bursting into flame as its full fuel tanks exploded, killing most people on the plane and some on the ground. There will be a public hue and cry, and policies will change at last, for here in America we set transportation policy by counting tombstones.

On January 15, 2009, at the controls after the bird strike, was a captain who was named best pilot in the 1973 graduating class of the U.S. Air Force Academy; who had been an F-4 Phantom II fighter pilot for seven years, as well as a flight leader in Europe and the Pacific who returned to the United States to lead flight war-games over Nevada; who had been a commercial pilot for twenty-nine years, spending 19,000 hours flying passenger jets; who had chaired the Airline Pilots Association's Safety Committee and aided the National

Transportation Safety Board in crash investigations; and who was a teacher of glider pilots, able to guide a powerless airliner over the George Washington Bridge and down to a level-winged landing on an urban river, with tall buildings packed with people all around.

Sullenberger described the experience to CBS News anchor Katie Couric: "Well, it was a normal climb out in every regard. And about ninety seconds after takeoff, I noticed there were birds, filling the entire windscreen, from top to bottom, left to right—large birds, close, too close to avoid."

When had he known there had been a bird strike? "Oh, you could hear them, as soon as they [struck] did. Loud thumps. It felt like the airplane being pelted by heavy rain or hail. It sounded like the worst thunderstorm I'd ever heard growing up in Texas. It was shocking." Couric asked: "When did you realize that these birds had seriously damaged the aircraft?" Sullenberger replied:

> When I felt, heard, and smelled the evidence of them going into the engines. I heard the noises. I felt the engine vibrations, of the damage being done to the engines. And I smelled, what I described at the time, and I still would, as a burned bird smell being brought from the engine area into the air conditioning system of the airplane.

Even though the plane continued to climb for several hundred feet after the strike, he knew the engines had failed:

> It was obvious to me from the moment that we lost the thrust, that this was a critical situation. Losing thrust on both engines, at a low speed, at a low altitude, over one of the most densely populated areas on the planet. Yes, I knew it was a very challenging situation.

The miracle on the Hudson gave uplift to a nation in need of a heroic story, but it should have also been heard as a "fire bell in the night," in Thomas Jefferson's phrase, warning us of danger. It should have caused the media and public to ask far more demanding safety questions than they did. The media's questions seemed largely limited to questions asked a half-century earlier by Boston newspaper reporters: "Can't we screen those jet engines over?"

The naïveté of the media in 1960 was understandable, a decade before high-volume jetliner travel had arrived—but not in 2009 when Sullenberger's plane was knocked out of the sky by birds, its jet engines dead silent with a 155 people on board.

As to screening over engines, the answer was no in 1960 and is no today. Much needs to be done to protect air travelers from collisions with birds, but, as discussed earlier, putting screens over jet engines is not one of the solutions.

Here are the questions that should have been asked aggressively of airport and other aviation industry personnel and the FAA on the days following the miracle on the Hudson: Why were Canada geese in the takeoff path of US Airways 1549—a flock of birds with wing spans of up to six feet? Why were the geese flying over the Cross Bronx Expressway? Were these migratory or nonmigratory Canada geese? (It turns out they were migratory, but they could well have been nonmigratory since New York's permanent goose population vastly outnumbers the transient migratory population.) Is it common for a flock of big birds to be in the flight path of a passenger jet near a major airport? How often does that happen? Why did well-tested aircraft engines fail on impact with geese? Why did the airliner have only two jet engines, if those engines can be so easily shut down by birds? If the plane had had three or four engines, would it have been more likely to come through the bird strike with a higher probability of some engine power available to help the pilot reach an airfield? Why wasn't Sullenberger aware there was a flock of geese in the sky, since he had taken off just ninety seconds earlier? Couldn't the air traffic controller have warned him that a flock of big birds was likely to be ahead of him on his ascent? If there been heavy hail over the Bronx or wind shear near LaGuardia, rather than a flock of geese, would not Sullenberger have been warned? Why do we track weather phenomena and not bird phenomena—especially when wildlife strikes on aircraft are the second-leading cause of aviation-related fatalities? With the aviation industry in such economic turmoil, will it continue to attract the best and brightest pilots? Will future Captain Sullenbergers or people of lesser talent be piloting our planes in the years to come?

Indeed, six weeks after his emergency landing, Sullenberger testified at an aviation safety hearing before the House Transportation and Infrastructure Committee, saying: "I do not know a single professional airline pilot who wants his or her children to follow in their footsteps." In recent years, his pay had been cut by 40 percent and his pension had been terminated, replaced by a federal Pension Benefit Guaranty Corporation's promise that he described as "worth pennies on the dollar." After 9/11, there was a wave of airline bankruptcies, and "the bankruptcies were used by some as a fishing expedition to get what they could not get in normal times." The problems, Sullenberger asserted, began with the deregulation of the airline industry in the 1970s.

There was, of course, a light flurry of questioning by the media following the landing on the Hudson, but it swiftly yielded center stage to the media's endless pursuit of human interest stories, in this case about those aboard US Airways 1549.

It is widely recognized by those working to reduce wildlife strikes on aircraft that there is no silver bullet, no single solution to the problem. After the miracle on the Hudson, the media should have picked up on this reality and pressed ahead with reporting on the need for a systemwide approach to safety, one that involves all stakeholders, to reduce strikes on aircraft. Transport Canada, a governmental agency that, among its other roles, acts as the FAA of Canada, has led the way in discussions of how to implement a systemwide safety approach. In *Sharing the Skies: An Aviation Industry Guide to the Management of Wildlife Hazards*, edited by Bruce Mackinnon and others, Transport Canada offers both insights into the problem of wildlife strikes and practical guidance for those seeking to make air travel safer. It is the single best book on the subject, and this chapter and the following draw mightily upon its major piece of wisdom: many parties need to work together to solve the problem. That is the same wisdom that led John Goglia, after the miracle on the Hudson, to call for a U.S. national summit on the problem of bird strikes.

There are twenty reported bird strikes per day across U.S. skyways. Since the FAA does not require pilots and mechanics to report wildlife strikes, even though the National Transportation Safety Board repeatedly has urged the agency to do so, the FAA is left to estimate the true scale of the problem, based on its calculation that only about 20 per-

An Eastern Airlines Lockheed L-188 with all of the original Eastern markings. Eastern Airlines was the first airline to receive delivery of the brand-new, much heralded Electra. The inaugural commercial flight of the L-188 took place on January 12, 1959. *Photo courtesy Lockheed, Wayne Cradduck Collection*

Stewardess and survivor Joan Berry, 22, from Prentice, Mississippi. *Photo courtesy Boston Public Library, Print Department*

Stewardess and survivor Patricia Davies, 23, from Jacksonville, Florida. *Photo courtesy Boston Public Library, Print Department*

Police, firefighters, and civil defense units from communities throughout Greater Boston, and as far away as Worcester, quickly arrive at the crash scene. Here, a Wakefield civil defense rescue boat is being carried to water's edge. *Photo courtesy Boston Public Library, Print Department*

A Coast Guard helicopter, ferrying the injured to land, on a return trip brings back a diver in a wetsuit to be lowered into Winthrop Harbor. *Photo courtesy Boston Public Library, Print Department*

"Hurrying through surf," read the caption of this October 5, 1960, *Boston Herald* photo. "Faces of these police and firefighters show the horror of the disaster as they race through surf to the Winthrop shore. Scores of civilians aided in the grim task." *Photo courtesy Boston Public Library, Print Department*

The *Boston Traveler* newspaper caption read: "Navy skin diver goes over the side of a rescue ship to check for bodies in the plane's wreckage. Two other divers stand in readiness at left." *Photo courtesy Boston Public Library, Print Department*

Deep sea diver James Rooney of Natick is helped down the ladder of a Navy launch as he prepares to search for remaining pieces of the plane. *Photo courtesy Boston Public Library, Print Department*

Arc lamps light the way as recovery efforts persist deep into the dark chilly night.
Photo courtesy Boston Public Library, Print Department

On October 5, the tail section of the aircraft is lifted out of the harbor and placed on a Navy barge to be taken, along with other parts, to a site in Hingham for reassembly—as the Civil Aeronautics Board tries to reconstruct events. *Photo courtesy Boston Public Library, Print Department*

Additional fragments salvaged by divers are piled onto the barge. Shown here are the center fuselage, the passenger ramp to the right, and the tail section in the background. Once the plane is reassembled, investigators will try to figure out what went wrong. *Photo courtesy Boston Public Library, Print Department*

Harvey Gorewitz, 18, of Dorchester was the first to be buried of 12 Marine recruits killed in the crash. He was laid to rest in dress blues as an honor guard of 10 Marines fired a volley in tribute. *Photo courtesy Boston Public Library, Print Department*

Frederick Abate, 18, of Quincy, seen here in a casual moment, was one of the Marine recruits killed in the crash. Sadly, his family and friends watched from the Logan observation deck as his plane took off and then crashed a minute later in Winthrop Harbor. *Photo courtesy Boston Public Library, Print Department*

Arthur Neumann, Bobbie Allen, and other members of the Civil Aeronautics Board hear from 43 witnesses across 3 days of hearings in January 1961. The hearings are conducted in the auditorium of the Massachusetts Air National Guard, barely a runway's length from the crash scene. *Photo courtesy Boston Public Library, Print Department*

The copilot of an incoming plane, Sheldon Lewis, describes to the CAB how Eastern Airlines 375 "fell off on the left wing" and plunged nose first into the bay. *Photo courtesy Boston Public Library, Print Department*

Ornithologist Roxie Laybourne of the Smithsonian Institution identified the charred feather remains in the plane's engines as those of starlings, and in so doing launched a new field in which she became the top expert: forensic ornithology. She also created the Smithsonian's world-renowned Feather Identification Lab. *Photo courtesy Smithsonian Institution Archives*

Captured in this picture, dated July 9, 1960, are happy days at the Cottage Park Yacht Club, one of the sites where Winthrop residents acquired the boating skills that helped save 10 lives in a crash the CAB called "nonsurvivable." *Photo courtesy Cottage Park Yacht Club*

cent of strikes are reported. On May 6, 2009, Senator Charles Schumer of New York announced that he was filing legislation that would make such reporting mandatory.

Even when a strike is reported, the FAA often lacks proper detailed information about the strike. A 2008 federal study of reported bird strikes from 1990 to 2007 revealed that only 43 percent indicated the type of bird, and just 26 percent identified the species of bird. So if only 20 percent of bird strikes are reported and just a quarter of reported strikes give the species, the FAA knows the species of bird involved in strikes in only five percent of all cases: one in twenty strikes. Yet wildlife biologists know that to develop effective programs to prevent bird strikes, information about the species of birds involved is necessary as well as data on where, when, and how the strikes occurred. As Schumer told reporters, "Complete reporting will enable us to pinpoint the real dangers, spot particular runways, time of day, flight patterns." He added: "It's not just a number, but what type of bird, where and when it occurred that will allow us to figure the best way to solve this problem."

By knowing the scale of the problem, defining it scientifically through data collection, much can be done to thwart wildlife strikes upon aircraft. The tools available today go far beyond the bird strike mitigation options available at Logan Airport in 1960, as described by Bernard Doyle, a member of the CAB team that investigated the accident: "We have a bird watch program out at the airport. They try to spot these things, and one of the standard [pieces of] equipment is a shot gun. They try to shoot them—especially the gulls—and scare off the birds. We also run a car down the runway, especially where the jets take off, and try to displace the birds."

It makes a huge difference to a systemwide safety approach to know if a particular airport's problems are starlings, gulls, sparrows, swallows, mourning doves, raptors, geese, ducks, or kestrels, and to understand the birds' patterns of behavior. Different birds are kept away by different methods.

Cutting grass to no less than six to ten inches in height is a good habitat control practice. If grass is higher than a bird's eye, birds cannot see predators or maintain interflock communication, so they feel uncomfortable and stay away. Also, if grass is too short, small mammals like rodents and chipmunks are able to race about, an invitation for diving raptors to hang out at the airport.

By the way, why would rodents be near an airport if airport businesses rigidly controlled garbage and trash collection and disposal, as they should? In fact, given intense noise pollution at airports, the types of enterprises that are willing to locate near an airport are those that don't care about noise—especially junkyards and city dumps.

We can begin to see the outlines of how a systemwide safety approach might work: it requires detailed information about the species and behavior of birds and other wildlife that are strike threats, habitat control, and the cooperation of government and businesses in the area. But that's only the beginning.

The Smithsonian Institution's Feather Identification Lab in Washington, has ornithologists eager to help identify birds involved in strikes upon aircraft, sometimes even from meager remains. Using DNA analysis, the Feather Lab can often identify the bird involved in a strike from "snarge," a term the lab's staff coined for the goop left behind after a bird strikes a plane in a high-velocity collision. The crew might have seen only a flash before impact and cannot identify the bird. The snarge or other remains—downy barbules, feet, talons, bones, wings, breast—can be gathered up and shipped to Washington, along with details about the strike, such as aircraft, location, altitude, damage done, and the like; ornithologists can then work their detective magic. But since the FAA does not mandate reporting of strikes, in the time-driven aviation industry, pilots and mechanics would rather not take the time to gather bird remains and ship them to Washington with a report. Still, if the FAA were to mandate reporting, the aviation industry would adapt, hiring people to aid with the task of reporting and passing the marginal added cost on to the public.

From time immemorial, safety initiatives have added time, cost, or both to business operations: the hamburger we eat would be cheaper if the Food and Drug Administration did not insist on inspections to insure our meat is healthy; cars would cost less if they didn't have to be equipped with seat belts and air bags; taxes would be lower if there were no traffic lights at intersections. The public decides the price of safety. On the plus side, new jobs are created when a safety measure is added to the cost of doing business; wages are earned that enter the economy and have a multiplier effect on it. In the United States today, a number of major airports have full-time wildlife biologists to oversee bird strike mitigation programs, both to help protect the public and, as we shall see, to protect the airports against lawsuits.

Even with the FAA's voluntary reporting system, the annual number of reported bird and other wildlife strikes in the United States more than quadrupled from 1990 to 2007, rising from 1,759 to 7,666. From 1990 until 2008, there were 89,000 strike reports filed with the U.S. Department of Agriculture, affecting civil aircraft and foreign carriers. These figures exclude strikes on military aircraft.

The FAA's analysis suggests that one reason for the quadrupling of reported bird strikes is an increased awareness among aviation personnel of mounting danger from wildlife strikes on aircraft. But the analysis also points to two other trends to explain the quadrupling: a sharp rise in aircraft operations (that is, movements of aircraft) and a spike in populations of hazardous wildlife, both in the skies and on the ground. Were the trends seen as vectors on an air traffic controller's radar screen, they would be deemed to be on a collision course—lights would be flashing, and alarms sounding.

A Brief History of Bird Strikes

The history of aviation and the history of bird strikes are virtually coterminous: almost as soon as people took to the skies in powered flight, they began slamming into birds.

The first recorded bird strike took place on September 7, 1905, near Dayton, Ohio. A short entry in the diaries of Orville and Wilbur Wright notes that Orville "flew 4,751 meters in 4 minutes 45 seconds, four complete circles. Twice passed over fence into Beard's cornfield. Chased flock of birds for two rounds and killed one which fell on top of the upper surface and after a time fell off when swinging a sharp curve." Given the season and location, it is likely that Orville struck a red-winged blackbird flying over Beard's field to feed on the ripe corn.

As mentioned earlier, the first recorded human death from a bird strike happened on April 3, 1912, when Cal Rodgers's aircraft crashed in the surf at Long Beach and he died—after a gull had jammed the flight controls of his spruce-framed, linen-covered biplane. At the dawn of powered aviation the circle of those involved was small: Rodgers had been taught to fly by Orville Wright. Since Rodgers's death, at least 223 other people have been killed in thirty-seven civil accidents involving birds, and sixty-three civil aircraft have been destroyed. In military aviation, since 1950 alone, at least 165 people have been killed and 353 aircraft have been destroyed, according to Transport Canada.

Since wildlife strikes are vastly underreported worldwide, the amount of financial losses and the numbers of accidents and even deaths are also underreported. When a plane crashes into a mountain in the Andes or a jungle in Central Africa, or vanishes over open ocean, do we know what brought it down? Birds are everywhere, high up in the Himalayas and down at sea level; over our planet's continents, islands, oceans, and seas. The Arctic tern migrates each year from the northern breeding grounds that give it its name to the southern waters off Antarctica, and then back again: 24,000 miles round trip, the longest migration of any earthly creature. The Arctic tern never lands, except to nest.

Financial losses from wildlife strikes to aircraft are estimated at $650 million a year in the United States alone. The Bird Strike Committee USA and the Bird Strike Committee Canada—which meet jointly annually and always include experts from the two governments, the military, the aviation industry, humane societies, and other organizations—report that, worldwide, airline companies lose one to two billion dollars a year to bird and other wildlife strikes.

For much of aviation history, bird strikes were deemed to be an act of God. Yet in the field of aviation, in public awareness, and in the law, there is a growing realization that, with a systemwide safety approach, wildlife strikes upon aircraft can be reduced. If they have not taken proper protective action, airports are being held legally liable for wildlife strikes, and many major airports are implementing wildlife strike avoidance programs of increasing sophistication. But, even with the best of these airport-based programs, the problem of wildlife strikes goes beyond the protections that can be offered by any one airport. The problem involves many stakeholders: local, city, and state governments; the airline industry; aircraft manufacturers; aviation unions; and bird protection organizations. Wildlife threats are starting to be seen as analogous to weather phenomena: natural, omnipresent, and to be closely watched, with warnings conveyed to pilots in a timely manner.

Interestingly, commercial airlines are far less flexible than the military in changing flight plans in the presence of bird activity. Military flights can often be scheduled to arrive or depart at times other than when bird life is particularly active—each morning and dusk, and in seasonal cycles. Worldwide bird migrations are locked into place by millennia-long patterns of the animals' behavior. While sharing knowledge across civilian and military sectors is valuable, Transport Canada notes, the difference in types of aircraft and flight standards means that the military aviation experience has little to teach commercial aviation, and vice versa. The military's advantage in scheduling and route selection makes it possible to avoid known zones and times of bird activity. Commercial airlines, however, must meet civilian demand: people travel when they must or when they wish.

But with better planning, improving technologies, the cooperation of a diverse array of stakeholders, and appropriate preventive steps, bird strikes can be reduced. Transport Canada's *Sharing the Skies* offers a vision of planes and birds both flying safely, if prudent and pragmatic initiatives are carried out by a range of parties. The agency's book is designed as a usable manual, similar to flight and other aviation manuals, and easily referred to by aviation professionals seeking to mitigate wildlife strikes while minimizing harm to wildlife. Published in a spiral binder, the book contains precise information that can be flipped to quickly. There is also an online version, which is constantly updated. And the book's copyright notice generously permits anyone to reproduce the publication "without permission provided the source is fully acknowledged."

While *Sharing the Skies* and the FAA's National Wildlife Strike Database and attendant analyses are principal sources I used for this chapter, other useful information is drawn from Bird Strike Committee USA. BSC-USA is a voluntary organization, begun in 1991 to improve the sharing of wildlife strike information among its members, who are drawn from the aviation industry, governmental agencies including the Department of Defense, and conservation groups. Also cited is Bruce Barcott's "Clearing the Air," which appeared in *Audubon*, especially regarding steps that ought to be taken to protect flights in and out of airports.

The Physics of a Bird Strike

Why are bird strikes so deadly? BSC-USA reports that if a twelve-pound Canada goose strikes an airplane traveling 150 miles per hour, it generates kinetic energy equal to a thousand-pound weight dropped from a height of ten feet. Transport Canada offers another vivid example. A four-pound bird striking an aircraft traveling at 288 miles per hour delivers an energy punch of 38,000 pounds. At an airspeed of 460 miles per hour, that energy punch soars to 100,000 pounds. A four-pound bird effectively becomes a 100,000-pound bird. The formula for kinetic energy is one-half the mass times the velocity squared. The velocity of which we speak is relative velocity: the sum of the velocities of bird and plane.

The halving of mass coupled with the squaring of velocity is why smart hitters in baseball choose a lighter bat to swing fast rather than a heavy bat that will be swung more slowly. All in all, when it comes to bird strikes, velocity makes collisions worse exponentially. This is why military aircraft, often required by their mission to fly fast at low altitudes—where most birds live and work—are more likely than civilian aircraft to suffer destructive damage and fatalities should a bird strike occur.

As an aside, were Ted Williams alive, there would be no better person with whom to discuss kinetic energy, airplanes, and bird strikes—recognized as baseball's greatest hitter, author of *The Science of Hitting*, a superb Marine Corps fighter pilot in two wars, and himself a near miss to be on Eastern Airlines Flight 375.

The U.S. Air Force has lost more fast-flying F-16 fighter jets to bird strike than any other aircraft, underscoring the role that velocity plays in the effects of bird strikes. Except for takeoff and landing, commercial airliners typically fly at high altitudes, where bird strikes are less common. But even if they are relatively safe at cruising altitudes, commercial airliners need to take off and land, which means passing through lower altitudes, inhabited by those hundred billion birds.

Below are the altitudes at which wildlife strikes occur; the figures include nonflying wildlife strikes, although these are a tiny portion of all wildlife strikes. Zero is ground level, although that can be high— Denver International Airport is at 5,141 feet; and the world's highest airport, in Bangda, Tibet, is at 14,219 feet—or low, as at Furnace Creek Airport, in Death Valley National Park, which is at minus 210 feet.

According to the FAA, the highest recorded bird strike on U.S. civil aircraft was 32,500 feet above ground level. Worldwide, Transport Canada reports the highest bird strike at 37,000 feet, which occurred in 1973 when a jetliner struck a Ruppell's griffon vulture in the skies above the Ivory Coast. Few bird species fly at that lofty altitude and, when they do, they usually are trying to fly over a very high mountain range—like the bar-headed goose that migrates over the Himalayas from its breeding grounds in Central Asia to its wintering area in India and other spots in South Asia, and then back again. Here are the figures from *Sharing the Skies*:

Altitude (in feet)	Percentage of Reported Incidents
0	40
1–99	15
100–299	11
300–499	5
500–999	7
1,000–1,499	5
1,500–3,999	10
over 4,000	6

Roughly sixty percent of wildlife strikes occur below 100 feet, seventy percent below 500 feet, and fewer than two percent above 10,000 feet. The altitude at which a damaging strike occurs is not necessarily the altitude a plane attains before visibly exhibiting signs of trouble. Eastern 375 and US Airways 1549 both continued to climb after devastating bird strikes. Eastern 375 did so because some engines continued to function, if erratically, until cascading troubles knocked the plane out of the sky less than a minute after takeoff. US Airways 1549 did so because after the engines failed, momentum pushed the aircraft along its vector of ascent until that momentum ebbed and gravity overcame it, with Sullenberger able to control only—and brilliantly so—the plane's path of descent: a deft glide down to a safe water landing on the Hudson River.

Today's Bird Strike Problem

From the first wintry flights at Kitty Hawk, North Carolina, on December 17, 1903, through the first lunar landing on the Sea of Tranquility on July 20, 1969, and our attainments in flight since, the possibility of loss of human life due to bird strike has never been greater than right now. Whether we take to the air in a wood-and-cloth biplane or by way of a rocket full of the newest technology, bird life will always be in our path. Our flyways are their flyways. There is no way around that fact, and we must find ways to live with it.

Sharing the Skies notes: "The bird-strike problem is a global one. Although the types of aircraft and species of birds involved in strike incidents vary from region to region, the population of some bird species and the number of aircraft sharing the skies is increasing every day—in every corner of the globe." The book warns that bird strikes are "a flight safety problem that's here to stay." Compared to October 1960, there are vastly more aircraft flights worldwide, so many passengers aboard airliners that only science-fiction writers could have imagined it fifty years ago. The Lockheed Electra L-188 carried some seventy-five passengers and crew, yet it was described in contemporary news stories as "a giant airliner." Today's Airbus A380 routinely carries 525 passengers, and it is certified to carry 800 or more in an all-economy-class configuration.

Since 1960 populations of large birds have skyrocketed, protected by international treaties pressed upon governments by bird protection groups. In the United States, large birds have benefited from the banning of DDT, a consequence of Rachel Carson's moving 1962 *Silent Spring*, and the cleaning up of many bays, harbors, lakes, ponds, rivers, and streams after the last fire on the Cuyahoga River.

Interestingly, growth in populations of large birds took place even as the populations of many small songbirds and shorebirds plummeted, "affected by climate change, habitat destruction, invasive species and disease," as Juliet Eilperin wrote in *The Washington Post* on March 20, 2009, after the publication of the U.S. Interior Department's longitudinal study "The State of the Birds." The department's analysis offered at best a mixed report after scrutinizing forty years of scientific data and citizen surveys. Among the country's worst affected areas were the Hawaiian Islands, which have lost seventy-one bird species since the first human inhabitants arrived in the archipelago.

In the matter of bird strikes upon aircraft, control of wildlife hazards at airports has become more difficult across the decades due to high urbanization near the world's major airports. For the first time in human history, half the planet's population lives in cities. Many airports, especially hub airports, are themselves small cities that offer ideal habitats for bird life: open grassy areas with water and food; no cats or dogs—in other words, safe, open places in otherwise crowded urbanized space.

Further, today many large airliners take off and land at airports in developing countries—not true in 1960—which are often in tropical environments rich with bird life. These airports are still racing to catch up to modern airports with more sophisticated bird strike mitigation programs, as might be found at major airports in North America and in northern Europe—even though these too need to improve their efforts.

Notably, in a quiet but dangerous revolution, there has been a shift in the U.S. commercial fleet away from planes powered by four jet engines to planes powered by two jet engines. It is far easier for a flock of birds to destroy engine power on a two-jet airliner than a three- or four-jet airliner. As NASA engineers well know, redundancy of systems can save lives.

In June 2008 the FAA, in cooperation with the Department of Agriculture, released a longitudinal analysis of "Wildlife Strikes to Civil Aircraft in the United States, 1990–2008," based on data from the FAA's National Wildlife Strike Database. The authors were top experts on wildlife strikes from the Department of Agriculture's Wildlife Services Program in Sandusky, Ohio: Richard A. Dolbeer, National Coordinator, Airport Wildlife Hazards Program, and Sandra E. Wright, the program's Wildlife Strike Data Base Manager.

While the report is driven by U.S. civil aircraft experience, it is indicative of global trends since half of the world's aircraft movements begin in the United States. The analysis cited three factors as having increased the threat to human health and safety from aircraft collisions with wildlife.

The first factor identified by the report is that "many populations of wildlife species commonly involved in strikes have increased markedly in the last few decades and adapted to living in urban environments, including airports. For example, from 1980 to 2006 the resident (nonmigratory) Canada goose population in the United States and Canada increased at a mean rate of 7.3 percent per year." As an example, 50,000 Canada geese now call Massachusetts their year-round home. Canada geese moved south to the area, found ample food, got fat, and decided to stay. The geese, unlike most avian species, can feed on grass—so they can be found loafing and eating along rivers, in parks, and on golf courses, athletic fields, median strips, and the grassy apron areas of airports.

In addition to Canada geese, other species of large birds have shown significant mean rates of annual increase, including wild turkeys (13 percent), turkey vultures (2.3 percent), American white pelicans (4.3 percent), double-crested cormorants (4.9 percent), sandhill cranes (4.7 percent) and bald eagles (5 percent). As with interest-accruing savings accounts, annual rates of population increase compound, boosting the total rapidly. For example, with a 13 percent annual rate of increase, the wild turkey population doubles every six years; the number of Canada geese, with a 7.3 percent annual rate of increase, doubles in under ten years. A startling thirteen of the fourteen bird species in North America with average body masses greater than eight pounds have shown significant population increases.

Sandra Wright delivered a paper at the 2007 joint meeting of the U.S. and Canadian Bird Strike Committees in Kingston, Ontario, showing that bald eagles, which hold a sanctified place in the American mind, had moved, in a few decades, from a threatened species to a threat to U.S. aviation. From fewer than 500 nesting pairs in 1970, the bald eagle population had increased to more than 10,000 pairs by 2007. Based on science and numbers, the birds were removed from the Department of the Interior's list of endangered species, but they continue to be protected by the U.S. Migratory Bird Treaty Act and other federal and state laws. Wright noted that there were eighty-four civil aircraft strikes by bald eagles between 1990 and 2006 in the United States. BSC-USA reports that about 90 percent of U.S. bird strikes are by species federally protected under the migratory bird treaty. Not all of those species are now in need of special protection: our emotions, not science or facts, often drive our laws.

The sharp rise in populations of large birds means that, in pilot argot, there is more "meat in the sky," capable of bringing down a sophisticated $200-million jetliner by shutting down its engines; damaging its radar-sensitive nose or its tail, wings, or rudder; or impairing its flight controls, the same thing that happened to Cal Rodgers's biplane in 1912.

Why large birds are a threat even to large modern airliners is revealed in the case of the Boeing 777—the world's largest twinjet, equipped with two huge, powerful turbofan engines. Each engine is more than nine feet across, easily accommodating the world's tallest man and nearing the diameter of the entire fuselage of a Boeing 737. Yet the big engines on the 777 can withstand the strike of only a single eight-pound bird. It is worth noting here that jet engines are required to be able to ingest a small bird and continue to function, but with large birds—up to eight pounds—they are only required not to explode, which could set off cascading catastrophic events. If the engine quietly shuts down, that's acceptable under current regulations; the engine does not have to continue to produce power. The engines of US Airways 1549 passed that test after the plane struck the geese; the only problem was that the airliner lost all power. It could only glide, ever downward.

In short, no jet engine in the world can ingest a full-sized Canada goose and continue to operate, as pointed out by John Goglia. Before the strike on US Airways 1549, Goglia was correctly asking: "One sixteen-pound Canada goose can destroy an engine; can you imagine what a flock of birds can do?" It's amazing what clarity of vision a sixteen-year-old can acquire while bringing up body parts from the murky waters of Winthrop Harbor.

While birds are the greatest wildlife hazard to aircraft, they are not the only source of danger. According to the FAA, birds are involved in 97.5 percent of reported strikes, terrestrial mammals in 2.1 percent, bats in 0.3 percent, and reptiles in 0.1 percent. Deer, coyote, and other terrestrial creatures are definitely a strike threat to aircraft on takeoff or landing. White-tailed deer in the United States increased from 350,000 early in the twentieth century to 17 million in the period leading up to the 2008 FAA study. A collision with terrestrial animals typically happens when an aircraft's landing gear hits a deer or other animal crossing the runway at night, when the creature cannot be easily seen by the pilot or air traffic control. Not something that we normally think about, yet still measurable, are nighttime strikes by flying mammals: bat strikes. And while neither terribly dangerous nor in the FAA study, one pilot reported a fish strike after a high-flying gull dropped a fish onto his windscreen.

The second factor in the growing risk of wildlife strikes identified by the FAA report is that "concurrent with the increase in populations of many large bird species, air traffic has increased substantially since 1980. Passenger 'enplanements' in the USA have increased from about 310 million in 1980 to 749 million in 2007 (3.3 percent per year), and commercial air traffic increased from about 18 million air-craft movements in 1980 to over 28 million in 2007." By 2020, U.S. commercial air traffic is expected to reach over 36 million move-ments.

The third and final factor is that, as noted above, "commercial air carriers are replacing their older three- or four-engine aircraft fleets with more efficient and quieter, two-engine aircraft. In 1969, 75 per-cent of the 2,100 passenger aircraft had three or four engines. In 2005, the USA passenger fleet had grown to about 8,200 . . . and only about 10 percent have three or four engines." Indeed, 90 percent of the airliners Boeing delivers today are twinjets.

The FAA added, in coolly scientific language: "This reduction in en-gine redundancy increases the probability of life-threatening situations resulting from aircraft collisions with wildlife, especially with flocks of birds. In addition, previous research has indicated that birds are less able to detect and avoid modern jet aircraft with quieter engines."

Why the switch to twinjets? When it comes to aircraft maintenance, twinjets are more reliable. Commercial aviation is an on-time, round-the-clock business. As passengers, we note with irritation when our transcontinental flight lands twenty minutes late, forgetting that not so many generations back, Americans crossed the country in Conestoga wagons and were happy to have arrived at all. Twinjets also save fuel, even if they put passengers at greater risk in case of a bird strike.

Commercial airlines make money when their planes are filled and flying, not when they are in a hangar being repaired. It's a matter of mathematics: the probability that a four-engine aircraft will need a repair on a single engine is higher than the probability that a two-engine aircraft will. In the airline industry, time on the ground disrupts the schedule, causing passenger inconvenience and loss of revenue as passengers make alternate plans; it also disrupts the complex schedule of getting the right flight crews into the right planes at the right time.

We have created a tight network of air travel, linking flight to flight through large hub airports; any disruption jostles a system that depends upon on-time arrivals and departures. When delays or missed connections occur, an airline's image suffers in an industry that is extremely competitive, with airline companies often operating close to the bone. So, why would an airline company choose twinjets? Because those planes are more likely to be in the sky and not on the ground being serviced. When passengers travel, they seldom think about equipment, paying more attention to routes and departure and arrival times—they do not even wish to think about whether there are occasions when two engines are not as safe as three or four. Yet it is worth considering that the president of the United States travels on Air Force One, a customized Boeing 747–200B series aircraft, which is a four-engine jet.

Two other design changes have contributed to the spike in bird strikes: the use of wide-body aircraft and quieter engines. These have decreased the time a bird has to escape if it happens to fly in front of, or gets overtaken by, an aircraft. Wide-body aircraft have been shown to be 50 percent more liable to bird strikes than narrow-body aircraft.

Quieter engines of course appeal both to passengers and to residents living under flight paths in and out of major airports. But quieter engines mean it is harder for birds to hear the jets, again reducing their escape time.

However, with the coming of quieter jets, airport birds might be less likely to go deaf. Dr. Allen Counter, a neurology professor at the Harvard Medical School in the 1980s, compared Logan Airport gulls to gulls in the quiet Monomoy National Wildlife Refuge on Cape Cod. He concluded that Logan gulls go deaf from jet roar, often flying into planes because they cannot hear them.

In the conclusion to its 2008 study, the FAA reported that "experts within the Federal Aviation Administration, the U.S. Department of Agriculture, and the U.S. Air Force expect the risk, frequency, and potential severity of wildlife-aircraft collisions to grow over the next decade." In other words, bird and wildlife strikes upon aircraft are here to stay. Hence, the problem of wildlife strikes needs to be dealt with, using the same ingenuity, persistence, and seriousness of purpose that put human fliers into the sky in the first place.

Perhaps it is apt at this juncture to turn to a matter of high irony— namely, that the bird that was the most direct inspiration for human flight, the turkey vulture, is now the bird most likely to cause costly damage in the event of a collision with an aircraft.

A turkey vulture circling over the Ohio River is said to have inspired the Wright brothers to build the world's first successful airplane. Turkey vultures have the ability to tower at 2,500 feet—to fly in a circular pattern, pretty much unworried, inasmuch as they have no predators in the sky, which contributes to their complacency in the presence of aircraft. Gregory McNamee, writing in the Britannica blog on December 17, 2008, on the 105th anniversary of first flights at Kitty Hawk, observes:

> Some of the brothers' ideas came from the books and technical papers they had read, to be sure. Others came from the close study of nature, and in particular of one species of bird: the turkey vulture. Of them Wilbur wrote, "My observations . . . lead me to believe that they regain their lateral balance, when partly overturned by a gust of wind,

by a torsion of the tips of the wings"—adjusting their feathers, in other words, to control the flow of wind over the wing.

As earlier noted, the first reported bird strike was logged by the Wright brothers in the summer of 1905 in Dayton, Ohio. On July 26, 2005, a century later, a turkey vulture struck the shuttle *Discovery*'s external fuel tank three seconds into launch over Cape Canaveral, Florida. The strike led to the death of the vulture but no damage to the shuttle. It is odd that the strike seemed to come as surprise to scientists at NASA since the Kennedy Space Center is located in a wildlife refuge, home to turkey and black vultures. A turkey vulture weighs three to five pounds and stands two to three feet tall; consider that the foam debris that struck the shuttle *Columbia* in 2003 on takeoff weighed only 1.7 pounds and led to the loss of the entire shuttle crew on reentry.

"A bird the size of a vulture can take out the shuttle if you hit it fast enough," reported Stephen Payne, a NASA test director, according to a June 7, 2006 posting on *USA Today*'s website: "We were asked to make sure we don't hit another vulture on the way up," so NASA introduced "battlefield noises" and baited traps in an effort to keep vultures far away from its Florida launch pad.

Love Them or Shoot Them Dead?
All evidence suggests that how we deal with bird strikes comes not from rational, considered policy; instead, all a-fumble, it seems to arise out of our deeply conflicted feelings about birds. Do we love birds or fear them? It might help to consider the question's constituent parts.

On the love side, here is a story from Winthrop Harbor, of all places, published in *The Boston Globe* on November 7, 2002:

> State and federal investigators have determined that the fatal shooting of a swan at Logan Airport in September was justified to keep the airspace clear for planes. Despite the findings, some Winthrop residents insist the shooting was unnecessary and say they are troubled by the use of live ammunition near their homes. Harbormaster Charles Famolare said he has received about 20 phone calls since the bird was shot on Sept. 13 by Massachusetts Port Authority officials. Many of the

callers expressed grief and anger at the death of the mute swan, which was raising four cygnets with its mate, Famolare said. Others were surprised to learn that Massport officials had used live ammunition so close to their homes, and worried aloud that an errant bullet could harm a child or other innocent passerby, he said.

While the objection to firing off live rounds close to a populated residential area seems reasonable, the objection to the killing of an adult swan seems to arise out of compassion for the mother swan and her cygnets. After all, a few miles from Winthrop Bay lies Boston's Public Garden, with its beautiful bronze statuary of the mother duck and brood of ducklings from Robert McCloskey's 1941 children's story, *Make Way for Ducklings*, set in Boston's Back Bay. Indeed, the Public Garden fences off from the public the annual spring nesting area of a swan couple until their eggs hatch. The nest sits next to a picturesque pond where, for more than a century, adults and children have enjoyed rides on a Boston cultural icon: the pedal-driven Swan Boats.

Contrast that love for birds with the fact that between 1991 and 1997, sharpshooters employed by JFK International Airport killed 52,235 gulls. JFK experiences 315 bird strikes a year, which should not be surprising given its location on seaside wetlands and its huge volume of air traffic. But we must not forget that the intruder is the airport, not the bird life around it. Birds inhabited those environs long before the airport was built, long before the Dutch ever thought of colonizing an outpost in New Amsterdam, which one day would become New York City. In fact, if any creature has suddenly infested the area, it is humankind: people and planes are now in the way of flying birds.

In the early days of aviation, many airports were built on seaside mud flats, just as Logan was in 1923, and later LaGuardia, Floyd Bennett Field in Brooklyn, Idlewild Airport (renamed JFK), and Crissy Field in San Francisco. The choice seemed ideal—aviators would have predictable winds and no trees or buildings in the way on takeoff or on landing. Indeed, parents take small children to the beach to fly kites for the same reasons, each child recapitulating, if you will, the flight experiments of Orville and Wilbur Wright in the windswept dunes of the Outer Banks.

When early airfields were built, no one knew that aviation would become the global industry that it did, with the masses able to travel by air, ticket prices driven down by volume, aircraft design, and competition. No one foresaw the need for large hangars that, in seaside airports, might sink into the mud. No one thought there was any reason to avoid centuries-old routes of migrating birds.

Even until June 3, 1995, airports were not legally responsible for damages incurred from bird strikes on takeoff or landing. But then everything changed. As reported by BSC-USA, an Air France Concorde landing at JFK ingested one or two Canada geese into the number three engine, ten feet above ground level. The engine suffered "an uncontained failure," with shrapnel from the number three engine then destroying the number four and cutting several hydraulic lines and control cables. The pilot managed to land safely, but damage to the plane was estimated at $9 million. The French Aviation Authority sued the Port Authority of New York and New Jersey, the parent of JFK, settling out of court for $5.3 million. No longer could an airport be protected from liability because a bird strike was an act of God. Such incidents were deemed avoidable if proper steps were taken by the airport.

Surely, their new liability confirmed to airport officials that the shoot-them-dead policy at JFK was a responsible course of action, necessary since human lives and costly aircraft were at stake. Yet that raises several questions we can rightfully ask of all stakeholders—the FAA, JFK, city, state, and national governments, the airlines, aviation unions, businesses in and around the airport, the wildlife sanctuary that borders the airport, conservation groups that protect birds no longer in need of protection, those who design and manufacture aircraft, the media and the public. First, could more have been done long ago to avoid the stark choice between dead people and dead birds? What did these stakeholders not do that placed the bird in the cross hairs of the shooter? And what can they—and we—do now to find a better way?

Cloud Physics
The U.S. Navy used to fund a brilliant cloud physicist who had what most people would call a dream job: to sit on some of the world's most beautiful beaches—first on Cape Cod, then in Hawaii—watch-

ing birds sail upon the ocean of air. Paid through Navy grants, the physicist watched gulls and terns ride warm updrafts up toward puffy white clouds, and then sink elegantly in downdrafts toward the white-tipped waves, the birds' wings making minor adjustments now and again so the birds could remain in the sky for long periods of time, minimum energy expended. The Navy could gather a lot of data about weather and aviation by having an especially smart person watch birds interact with mobile packets of air, riding imaginary elevators up and down. Birds are experts in fluid mechanics, with Mother Nature their skilled teacher, and we are the great plagiarizers. We watch, steal, and adapt.

Although humans today sail successfully upon the ocean of air, with our aircraft capable of vast speed that far outstrips any bird's, we do not fly as adroitly as birds. Our planes lack their maneuverability, their prudent use of energy, and the stealth coupled with quickness of great avian hunters. We are left to wonder, even after more than a century of human flight: Did God love birds better than people to give them such gifts? A sure sign of their special place is that birds are the sole creatures on earth with feathers, which allow them to do amazing things—such as changing the contour of their bodies to be as aerodynamic as the flight moment requires. A swan has 25,000 feathers; even the tiny hummingbird has a thousand.

Our finest aeronautical engineers try to build into aircraft designs the ideas they find in bird life. In PBS's "Raptor Force," researchers mounted miniature cameras on raptors to reveal why peregrine falcons, golden eagles, and red-tailed hawks are envied by the hottest fighter pilots in the U.S. Air Force. The F-22 fighter jet, nicknamed "the raptor," is the world's fastest-turning airplane, equipped with wings and tails that morph, mimicking a raptor's. Still, as New York City's Channel 13 pointed out in a press release about the PBS show, "the peregrine falcon's anatomy is so advanced that, were it the same size as the F-22, the bird would outmaneuver the jet in a dogfight." This is why some top-gun pilots say that in the next life they wish to be raptors.

In another example of aeronautical engineers' use of ideas from birds, Channel 13 observed that the F-117 Nighthawk's stealth was inspired by the owl, the quietest bird in flight. The Nighthawk has a special coating that reduces the aircraft's radar profile to that of a small bird. It is able to attack undetected.

Airport Vulnerability
Despite our love, admiration, and emulation of birds, we are still quite willing to shoot them dead by the tens of thousands at airports, in the case of even possible trouble between bird and plane. You seldom hear airport officials admit that it was not smart to have built airports by the sea or along migratory bird routes. Officials do not call attention to their airport's problems with wildlife hazards for fear of losing business.

After the miracle on the Hudson, pressure mounted on the FAA to publish reports of bird strikes by airport. The FAA tried to avoid being required to release the information. But the media began to ridicule the FAA for shilling for the aviation industry, and the Secretary of Transportation finally stepped in to force the FAA to release the data.

Why did the FAA resist? As *Sharing the Skies* observes: "Some industry stakeholders believe strike reporting creates information liabilities, raising public fears about the potential for strike-related accidents." Others had a different explanation: the FAA is too cozy with the aviation industry and is now the fox in charge of protecting the chickens.

While no airport wishes to be identified as subject to wildlife strikes, no federal agency has a right to suppress travel safety statistics. Once made public, the FAA and the aviation industry have every right—in fact, a responsibility—to set the statistics in context for the public. After the release of the information, they did so with mixed success, which was evident in news stories at the time. CBS News, for example, in a report dated April 24, 2009, presented the raw data on airport bird strikes as follows:

> Airplane collisions with birds have more than doubled at 13 major U.S. airports since 2000. Denver, Houston, Chicago O'Hare and New York's Kennedy airport reported the most wildlife strike incidents, according to Federal Aviation Administration data released for the first time Friday.

The FAA list of wildlife strikes, published on the Internet, details more than 112,387 incidents (101,995 civil and 10,392 military) since 1990, reports CBS News producer Carter Yang. The incidents involved 460 species of birds and other various animals such as deer and cows. Of the 112,387 incidents, 3,001 or 2.67 percent caused "substantial damage" to the aircraft, Yang reports. There were 28 cases since 2000 in which a collision with a bird or other animal such as a deer on a runway was so severe that the aircraft was considered destroyed. The total number of reported strikes rose from 2,074 (the lowest number on record) in 1990 to 9,897 (the worst year on record) in 2007. Last year, 2008, the number dropped to 8,758, Yang reports.

About the only meaningful information in that jumble of statistics is that wildlife strikes have doubled since 1990 at thirteen major U.S. airports—which actually indicates that bird strike reports rose sharply at these airports, though the number of strikes probably increased as well. But what is a major airport? Are these thirteen the very busiest airports? Did the statistics not double at any major airport? And if not, why, and which airports were in this category? Another important question is did airport traffic at the thirteen airports double over the same time period? More takeoffs and landings mean more chance of bird strikes. The FAA needs to contextualize the numbers so the media and the public can make sense of them.

The Gold Standard

As a measure of wildlife strikes, the gold standard is incidence of the strikes. As Bruce Barcott wrote in *Audubon*, the "batting average" for the aviation industry is wildlife strikes per 10,000 movements of aircraft. For the United States overall, he notes: "In 1990 it was 0.53, or one strike for every 20,000 flights. By 2007 it had tripled, to 1.75." With any news story about wildlife strikes at airports, the media should ask for the batting average and whether that figure has changed over time. An observer then can make fair comparisons among airports.

CBS at least included some information that set in context why JFK had a higher volume of bird strikes than other airports: "Kennedy, the nation's 6th busiest airport, is located amid wetlands that attract birds." But the news story still failed to provide the number of strikes per 10,000 movements, so we can't tell if JFK is more or less safe than other airports.

In sheer volume of serious incidents, JFK did top the FAA's list (although it did not necessarily have the highest batting average). On April 25, 2009, Michael Sniffen of the Associated Press reported that JFK had had at least thirty incidents in which aircraft were "either substantially damaged or destroyed by birds since 2000." Sniffen also reported that Sacramento International Airport had had at least twenty-eight such incidents, adding the important information that the airport, "the nation's 40th busiest, lies beneath the Pacific Flyway used by millions of geese, swans, ducks, cranes, raptors, and other birds that migrate and stop to feed on crops in farms next to the airport."

When setting the JFK bird strike experience in context, an issue worthy of significant consideration is that, in addition to sharpshooters that kill birds, JFK also has a sophisticated bird strike mitigation program in place—wildlife biologists and others work aggressively to insure that planes fly in and out of the airport safely. Of course, JFK and other poorly sited airports at threat from wildlife hazards are likelier, far sooner, to put into place new approaches and technologies to mitigate strikes than airports that currently have less of a problem. Airports with a short history of wildlife strikes can find that their safe situation degrades rapidly when real estate developers remove native habitat, forcing birds and animals closer to the airport, where there is inviting open space and no plan or tools in place to deal with the incursion.

The borough of Queens, New York, is home to two major airports: JFK and LaGuardia. On May 7, 2009, Stephen Geffon of the *Queens Chronicle* reported that FAA data showed that, from January 1990 to November 2008, JFK had reported 1,811 bird strikes, the most for any airport in the nation. LaGuardia had 954. Geffon pointed out that JFK is located near the Jamaica Bay Wildlife Refuge—9,000 acres of islands and salt marshes and home to 330 bird species; a breeding ground for the gulls, geese, and mourning doves responsible for most of the strikes at the airport. Indeed, JFK actually shares a shoreline with the wildlife refuge. Senator Schumer, Geffon reported, was advocating that millions of federal dollars be put into bird strike mitigation efforts at airports in New York and elsewhere. Geffon noted that the Port Authority of New York and New Jersey had a $3-million, five-year contract to deploy falcons at JFK to drive away the gulls. In Geffon's story, one sees something of a systemwide safety approach at work: many parties across the public and private sectors are cooperating so that humans can safely share the skies with avian life. For example, a senator calls for more government money to protect our airports from wildlife strikes; the Port Authority pays for falcons, a natural gull predator, to scare off gulls to reduce strikes; the Jamaica Bay Wildlife Refuge announces it is being careful not to build up its avian population. Had the City of New York not thoughtlessly established several landfills near JFK, that too would have helped. When Hitchcock was making *The Birds*, most of the filming of birds was actually done at dumps because such sites attract lots of birds.

In the months following the emergency landing of US Airways 1549, the Port Authority announced it was installing two Canadian-made Accipiter bird radar systems at JFK to track the course, speed, and altitude of birds. Both the manufacturer and aviation experts acknowledge that current bird radar systems could not have prevented the plane's collision with the Canada geese at 3,000 feet. In a September 11, 2009, article in the *Queens Chronicle*, Lisa Fogarty quoted Tim Nohara, Accipiter's CEO, as saying: "At 3,000 feet, the Flight 1549 incident was an outlier." He added: "The story has such endurance that it has created public awareness, which is great. But the problem we're trying to solve is at airports and on airport property." To put a final fine point on the matter, he stated: "The number one use of Avian radars is not to detect geese at 3,000 feet, which is rarely the cause of such tragedies, but to track them below 500 feet, where the majority of bird strikes occur—both during take-off and landing." Fogarty reported that Accipiter is in the process of developing "more advanced three-dimensional radar technology that uses multi antennas."

A few months earlier, on July 9, 2009, the Associated Press reported that Logan Airport, also known for its aggressive bird mitigation program, had begun testing the bird radar system used by the U.S. Air Force at a number of bases to protect its fighters, and now also by NASA to protect its shuttles: the Merlin avian radar system created by DeTect Inc., of Panama City, Florida. The Merlin bird radar, according to the AP report, "allows real-time tracking of birds as small as a starling and as far away as nearly five miles. A spinning blade of horizontal radar provides an airport overview, while vertical radar scans a specific runway. Birds appear as red dots, with tails indicating their flight path."

Logan was also planning to test the Accipiter avian radar system. Incidentally, according to Sniffen, the FAA data on bird strikes by airport showed Logan as having twelve serious incidents, ranking it eleventh in the country. Seattle-Tacoma International Airport has been the FAA's primary bird radar test site since 2006, with Sea-Tac now testing two different avian radar systems. Chicago's O'Hare and Dallas–Fort Worth are also among airports installing bird radar systems.

It should be made clear, however, that it will take years until the kinks have been worked out of new bird radar systems. Recall that radar was invented to track large objects—planes and ships—not small ones. An example of an issue being worked on by engineers is how to differentiate a cluster of birds from cells of rain. Even when bird radar systems are perfected, airports, pilots, and the FAA will need to puzzle out how to use the information in an efficient and effective manner, so as not to overload pilots and air traffic controllers who are already intensely busy at points of takeoff and landing. There are also problems of cost and choice: the radar systems are extremely expensive, and there are several to choose from. Purchase decisions must be made carefully, especially when dealing with new technologies still in development, upon which hundreds of lives and multimillion-dollar aircraft may depend.

"How Many Geese Did You Gas Today?"

On July 7, 2009, the Port Authority's website announced that the agency would be paying half the cost of rounding up geese and removing them from forty city properties located near LaGuardia and JFK. The roundup would be contracted out to the U.S. Department of Agriculture, which would then euthanize the birds.

Birdstrike.com, a website posting vital news about bird strike issues, reported that dozens of protesters had gathered outside Port Authority offices to protest the killing of the 2,000 geese, which would be rounded up during molting season, when they cannot fly. The protesters chanted, "How many geese did you gas today?" recalling the antiwar chant aimed at President Lyndon Johnson during the Vietnam War: "Hey, hey, LBJ, how many kids did you kill today?" One protester held a sign that read: "Gassing is not a long-term solution." A Port Authority spokesman, Stephen Sigmund, with a gift for rhyming language, commented: "Our responsibility is to think about safety for people before peace for geese." Edita Birnkrant, director of Friends of Animals in New York City, which led the protest, was quoted as saying: "This is a terrible precedent to set, that anytime there is a problem with wildlife—to just slaughter them is not a way to solve the issue." She added: "The Humane Society of the United States says that Canada geese can be effectively managed with nonlethal techniques like aversive conditioning, egg addling and landscape management."

Once again, the conflict: love the birds or kill them.

Birds in Film: A Cosmic Double Feature

Perhaps the conflict set out in this chapter can be seen more sharply if differently framed. Imagine a lofty intelligence from a distant galaxy learning of intelligent life on earth—that would be the humans—and of the colorful, abundant bird life in the lower atmosphere. That lofty intelligence, wondering how the 6.8 billion humans feel about the 100 billion birds fluttering around them, using Google cosmic, pulls up from our culture the two most acclaimed, wildly popular films ever made about birds: *Winged Migration* (2001) and *The Birds* (1963). Then the lofty intelligence sits down with a galactic-size box of popcorn and screens the two films as a double feature. What might that lofty intelligence learn about how humans feel about birds?

First, *Winged Migration*.

The film—a little more than a documentary, but not quite a drama— is so beautiful that it makes humans want to weep at the splendor and valor of gorgeous migrating birds. Twice a year, migratory birds traverse giant arcs of our planet—sometimes, as in the case of the Arctic tern, from one end of the globe to the other and back again. The film follows a rich variety of migratory birds, sometimes through journeys of thousands of miles, beset with danger: across continents and over trackless oceans, wind-lashed islands, blazing deserts, and snow-covered mountains. The birds must overcome severe weather, exhaustion, and famine. Their quest is a simple one: for survival, food, and safe nesting areas. But they have only a short time to spend in their safe haven before they must take to the skies again to journey back from whence they came. "Heaven is ephemeral," the narrator tells us.

Part of the sound track includes the birds' heavy rhythmic panting in flight, reminiscent of Gregorian chant. But in fact the birds were dubbed by humans: the rhythmic panting was scored in musical notation and performed in a studio by a chorus.

The birds' noble journeys in *Winged Migration* are marred only by humans; it is clear their world would be a better place if there were no people. In virtually every frame of film, the birds are seen in a sacred light. Even starlings, in a tight flock of tens of thousands, are seen performing their amazing aerial ballet set against a crimson sky at sunset (like the one at Logan on October 4, 1960); in the foreground, waterfowl rest picturesquely on a pond. Heading south across North America, the heroic migrating birds are shockingly felled from the sky by hunters' shotgun blasts. In fact, the shotgun, originally called a fowling piece, was invented for precisely such use in the killing fields of the skies. In the film, hunters trick exhausted birds with decoys and use trained bird dogs to drive birds out of the high, safe grass in the wetlands and into panicked flight, so as to give the hunters a clear shot.

In Europe, red-breasted geese in migration land in a dark, satanic Eastern European industrial city; iron, steel, heavy machinery, open fires, smokestacks, and air pollution are everywhere; factories dump chemicals into waterways. One goose must be left behind by its comrades: the bird's feet are stuck in industrial sludge. In actuality the scene was staged, with innocuous substances mixed together to create the look of sludge.

Thirsty Canada geese, passing over the red-tinted high plains of the southwestern United States, stop and drink what surely are poisonous fluids leaking out of a rusting old truck, abandoned along a road by humans. We witness a panzer division of hay-cutting machines roll across a field, blades flashing, ready to chop up any birds in their path. There is one scene that surely led to cheers in some movie theaters: in it, we see a boat on the Amazon, piled high with wooden cages filled with desolate captured monkeys and toucans to be sold by poachers; a clever blue toucan, using his beak, reaches through the bars, unlocks the door, and escapes to freedom.

The only humans in *Winged Migration* who show any kindness toward birds are those in the shadows of life: a very elderly woman and a small boy. All other humans are shown as either cruel or horribly thoughtless.

On the DVD, the bonus feature on the making of the film concludes with Nguyen Kakiu's poem, "In Our Next Lifetime," which includes this sentiment: "In our next life we'll take care not to be humans / We'll be two wild geese flying high in the sky." In *Winged Migration*, our love, compassion, and empathy are with the birds, and we are perplexed that humans could be arrayed against these beautiful, gifted creatures.

Now, halfway through the box of popcorn, the lofty intelligence starts to watch the second half of the double feature, doubtless expecting similar expressions of love and admiration for earth's beautiful birds. Not so.

Second, *The Birds*.

A beautiful blonde, Melanie Daniels (Tippi Hedren), drives up the coastal road in her open sports car, sixty miles from San Francisco to the idyllic northern California town of Bodega Bay. She is on a flirtatious mission to deliver a pair of lovebirds to a handsome eligible bachelor, Mitch Brenner (Rod Taylor), whom she just met in a San Francisco pet shop. The ominous future is prefigured when Melanie, after delivering the lovebirds, is inexplicably attacked by a seagull. There are several increasingly foreboding events—a large seagull smashes headlong into the front door of schoolteacher Annie Hayworth (Suzanne Pleshette) and dies; the chickens in Bodega Bay mysteriously stop eating. At an outdoor birthday party for Cathy (Veronica Cartwright), Mitch's little sister, birds mass on a jungle gym and suddenly launch a vicious attack on the children. The children are knocked to the ground, with birds pecking at their heads and faces. Later, Cathy asks, "Why are they doing this? Why are they trying to kill people?"

As the film's trailer says: "They're coming. They're coming. The birds massed by the thousands, and tens of thousands. Why? What was their evil intent?"

The assaults in Bodega Bay mount in number and ferocity. One man's home is attacked, and Mitch's mother (Jessica Tandy) finds him dead, eyes gouged out by big birds that smashed through his bedroom window by night and killed him.

The local people try to figure out what's happening. An eccentric, elderly amateur ornithologist, Mrs. Bundy (Ethel Griffies), scoffs as Melanie describes the frenzied attack on innocent children. "A bird war? Impossible," Mrs. Bundy says. "Birds are not aggressive creatures. They bring beauty into the world. It's mankind who makes it difficult." She doubts that "a few birds are going to bring about the end of the world." Melanie replies coolly, "There are not just a few birds. There are gulls, crows, and swifts." Incredulous, Mrs. Bundy says: "I have never known different species of birds to flock together. . . . If that happened, why we wouldn't have a chance. How could we possibly hope to fight them?"

As the debate continues, a well-dressed businessman, passing through town, chimes in: "If you ask me, we should wipe them all out. The world would be better off without them. All they do is make a mess of everything. Who needs them?" Hitchcock sees to it that the businessman dies a violent death, as his car explodes in flames.

Later, the Brenners' home comes under a full-scale coordinated attack, with big birds pecking their way through a thick front door, and a huge flock of small birds shooting down the chimney and entering the Brenners' living room. At some point, Melanie realizes what is going on, and says, half to herself: "It's an uprising of the birds . . . 'Why should humans rule?' the birds ask themselves."

Like guerrilla fighters, the birds attack, regroup, and attack again. In a moment of quiet, the Brenner party decides to escape. They make their way carefully and slowly out of the house, with the birds all about their feet and perched all around them on the house. They get in Melanie's sports car and edge away from the house. They have learned from radio reports that other, smaller bird attacks have occurred. On the radio there is talk of bringing in the army. Who knows what the future holds?

The car makes its way slowly down the coastal road, silhouetted against the massed birds of Bodega Bay; the birds are gathered, sitting, waiting. What is their evil intent? That is the film's ambiguous ending.

But Hitchcock's original ending, which proved too expensive to film, had no ambiguity: it was to be a full-screen shot of the Golden Gate Bridge completely covered by birds, showing the birds in possession of the symbol of San Francisco—evil and unstoppable.

In watching these two films, what does the lofty intelligence learn about humans' attitudes toward birds? Surely, that we have dramatically conflicted feelings about birds. We love them, adore them, fear them, and want to kill them.

In 1963, millions flocked to the cinema to watch birds attack the good people of Bodega Bay. In a 1994 sequel, *The Birds II: Land's End*, a straight-to-television film, birds attack humans once again for no apparent reason. Surely millions of people will flock to watch a remake of *The Birds* due for release in 2011, slated to star Naomi Watts.

Why our apparently unremitting obsession with *The Birds*? Does the fear aroused in a darkened theater emanate from the irrational part of our brain? And what precisely causes the fear: guilt? Bad memories of experiences with birds that the most primitive part of our brain protectively recalls?

Until October 4, 1960, Eastern Airlines had flown 40 million passengers two and a half billion miles without a single fatality. It stretches credulity to believe that small birds like starlings, each weighing less than three ounces, can kill an airliner and mar such a sterling safety record. But that is what happened. And of course it is the limits of credulity that Hitchcock explores in *The Birds*.

When Hitchcock made the movie, he surely knew of the 1960 downing of the Boston Electra by bird strike—a story that had received worldwide attention—but his film is based on Daphne du Maurier's 1952 novelette, *The Birds*.

In du Maurier's story, set on England's Cornish coast—three hundred miles of coves and golden beaches not unlike California—birds attack a farm family and perhaps all of Europe, sending planes crashing. Fiction, like dreams, often gives form and visibility to our unconscious life, as Freud and Jung knew and tried to explain to us. As humankind reaches for the sky, one of our deep-seated fears might be that we have intruded upon space that God has reserved for others, and that retribution is heading our way. Why else do the birds of du Maurier and Hitchcock seem to operate out of resentment?

For sixty million years, birds ruled the sky. Humans wandered out of Africa only sixty thousand years ago, and we reached the sky just a century ago. Perhaps on some days, birds do think we should have stayed where we belong, on terra firma, where they can watch our antics at a safe distance, from a bird's-eye view.

While many Americans justifiably complain that Canada geese have infested our skies, green spaces, and riverbanks, and as we press forward with plans to kill birds that loaf around airports, let's not lie to ourselves. We, not Canada geese or any other birds, have infested—even fouled—a goodly portion of the planet's lands, seas, and skies. So, in parsing blame for bird strikes, it might be wise to turn to the planet's greatest poet, Shakespeare, by way of the words of his Cassius: "The fault, dear Brutus, is not in our stars, but in ourselves."

If nonhuman life on earth could weep, it would do so at the failure of the Zero Population Growth movement of the late 1970s and early 1980s. The movement argued that humankind's population should only replace itself, not increase. Had it succeeded, our environmental problems would be far diminished—and, with fewer planes in the sky, there would be less chance of bird-plane collisions.

Today, in the United States alone, there are 64 million takeoffs and landings per year. Until the miracle on the Hudson, we pretty much believed that birds should simply get out of our way when we fly; in fact, most of us still believe that. Yet there are fifteen times more birds on earth than people, and while earth is our home, it is theirs too.

The day after US Airways 1549's emergency landing, Jonathan Rosen, author of *The Life of the Skies: Birding at the End of Nature*, wrote a piece for *The New York Times* website called "Room for Debate: a Running Commentary on the News." He commented: "We have reached the moment in our civilization when the technology that endangers the wild world is necessary to save it—much in the same way that the Florida Everglades, destroyed 100 years ago by the Army Corps of Engineers, is in part maintained by pumps and sluices that are today constructed by the Army Corps of Engineers." We will explore this topic further—the use of latter-day technology to help us more safely share the skies—but first, more about those starlings and the second worst air tragedy in history caused by bird strike.

Starlings Again: The Second Worst Bird Strike Disaster
European starlings can swarm in the millions and fly wing-to-wing at forty miles per hour, executing tight turns with balletic grace, in rapid succession, one bird never striking another. Even Wayne Gretzky, the greatest and quickest ice hockey player ever to have played the game, would admire the starlings' ability en masse to spin and reverse, dodge and elude—to avoid the suddenly appearing tree, building, or flying buttress. So why on a bright, clear October afternoon in 1960 did a flock of 10,000 to 20,000 starlings slam straight into the engines of the Boston Electra, then traveling at a comparatively slow takeoff speed? Did they not see it? Or was there—preposterous—intentionality as with the birds of du Maurier and Hitchcock? Is the starling not only a widespread nuisance but also a terrorist? Impossible. Still, it is curious that during more than a century of human flight—involving billions of aircraft movements and many tens of billions of people in our skyways—the second worst air tragedy caused by bird strike, to date, was also caused by starlings, rather than any other one of the 10,000 species of birds.

Here is a summary of that second terrible, tragic crash caused by starlings, based mostly on the formal investigation by committees from the Royal Netherlands Air Force, the Belgian Air Force, and local and national authorities in the Netherlands.

At about 6:00 p.m. on July 15, 1996, after a number of uneventful flights that day, a Belgian Air Force C-130 Hercules—a four-engine turboprop built by Lockheed—with thirty-seven passengers and a crew of four aboard was landing at its final stop, Eindhoven Air Base, in the Netherlands. Most of the passengers were members of the Royal Netherlands Army's Brass Band, which had given several performances in Italy and was returning to Eindhoven; their tubas, trumpets, slide trombones, and dress uniforms packed away on the burly C-130, a type of aircraft used in military and civilian operations worldwide for a half-century. The C-130 had a fine safety record.

As the plane approached the landing field, the crew spotted a large number of birds flying up from the top of the runway and began to execute a missed approach (with the intention of approaching a second time) to avoid the birds. Estimates put the flock at 500 to 600, mostly starlings but with a few lapwings mixed in. During the missed approach, a large number of birds struck the cockpit and left wing. The aircraft veered to the left and rapidly lost altitude. The tip of the left wing hit the ground, piercing an exterior fuel tank; fuel began to flow from the tank to the ground and caught fire. The plane slid across the ground, with the propellers of the number one, two, and three engines breaking off successively, until the aircraft came to a standstill and burst into flames—which enveloped the forward section. While air traffic control knew there were passengers on board, base fire command somehow and tragically remained unaware of them, assuming only the crew was aboard. With the forward section wrapped in jet-fuel flames, the firefighting unit believed the crew had lost their lives and focused its attentions on extinguishing the fire, which it did quickly and in a tactically correct manner.

The cause of the crash was determined to have been a collision with 150 birds, according to the Royal Netherlands Air Force's Albert de Hoon and Luit Buurma. The investigation revealed dozens of birds lodged in three of the plane's four engines. All forty-one people aboard appeared to have survived the crash but, as a result of the fire, most on board died—with a key factor being impact damage that precluded opening any of the plane's doors from the inside.

The official investigation determined that the rescue of crew and passengers "could have been initiated at least 25 minutes earlier. Had this been the case, the number of casualties could possibly have been fewer." The cause of death in the vast majority of cases, if not all of them, was toxic fumes.

De Hoon and Buurma learned that in the weeks leading up to the crash, the base staff had planned to cut the bird control unit in half, from two people to one; the day after the crash, the unit's staff was doubled instead. The investigators also determined that, as the Hercules was on landing approach, the birds were out of view of the control tower—concealed in the grass along the runway. The grass had been mowed several days earlier, but the deep layer of clippings left on the ground made it difficult for the control tower to see the birds. The birds suddenly flew into the path of the Hercules. Later, periodic studies by the bird control unit—done even a couple of years after the crash—showed 300 birds living at the airbase in summer and 150 in winter; their presence was the result of ongoing problems of water drainage and mowing of runway areas. Once these problems were dealt with, the number of birds declined—a reminder that the first line of defense against bird strikes at airports is always habitat control.

Awareness of our conflicted feelings about birds helps to keep the rational in control of the irrational, which often quickly translates into bringing in the guns or gassing the geese. Killing birds should never be ruled out, but it should truly be a last resort, especially since it often shuts down efforts to find more permanent, long-range solutions. At Eindhoven Air Base, both a military and a civilian airport, sharpshooters could have been deployed daily to pick off starlings and lapwings at the airfield. Instead, even though it took time, the base staff figured out how to deal with their water drainage problems (no surprise, given that they are Dutch) and learned to keep the runway area grass mown and quickly remove the clippings.

Had the base's bird control unit numbered four people from the start, perhaps the base staff would have solved their problems before a brass band was silenced and a Hercules aircraft destroyed.

6 Sharing the Skies: The Solutions

As long as birds reach for the heavens, our imagination will soar along with them. —The narrator of the documentary film *Birds*

Making airports safer when it comes to bird strikes, as Bruce Barcott aptly observes, requires an "ornithologist's knowledge of bird behavior, high-tech radar equipment, labor intensive ground observation, and some old-fashioned detective work." And to make all of aviation—our skyways as well as our airports—safer from bird strikes requires still more. Anyone seeking long-term solutions to reducing bird and other wildlife strikes eventually returns to the systemwide safety approach advocated by Transport Canada, for the reasons cogently expressed in a single paragraph in *Sharing the Skies*:

> Careful use of state-of-the-art wildlife-management techniques and current technology to detect hazardous bird movements can provide timely information and warnings to flight crews. Enhanced bird- and mammal-impact protection of aircraft and engines can have a measurable effect on reducing the risk and associated costs—both human and financial—that bird and mammal strikes incur.

Since there is no silver bullet that can eliminate wildlife strikes, all we can do is effectively manage the risk of wildlife strikes so as to reduce their incidence and severity. Transport Canada offers a three-tiered plan to do so. But before we discuss that plan, let us cast an eye back at the good that came out of the crash of the Boston Electra—in addition to the miracle on Winthrop Harbor, when ten people survived a nonsurvivable crash. Following the crash, the FAA finally took action to develop minimum bird ingestion standards for turbine-powered engines, spurred on by the remarkable Roxie Laybourne at the Smithsonian's Museum of Natural History, in Washington, who positively identified the charred remains and feathers in the Electra's engines as those of starlings. In so doing, Laybourne launched a whole new field in which she became the top expert: forensic ornithology.

The aircraft industry strengthened turbine blades and jet-fighter canopies to better withstand bird strikes. Airports launched the first campaigns to make their property less inviting to birds: clearing away vegetation; requiring strict rubbish removal; using shotguns, propane cannons, and pyrotechnics to frighten off flocks; deploying birds of prey, both real and artificial; chasing off birds by dog patrols, with border collies and German shepherds the breeds of choice; and, yes, shooting birds dead.

Eventually, radar-based systems began to be developed, to give real-time warnings to pilots of potential bird strikes, although there remained the nagging problems of speed of data upload, adequate resolution of small objects, distinguishing birds from rain cells, and pinpointing the position of birds in three dimensions. For the driver of a car or the skipper of a boat, pinpointing an object in two dimensions works fine, but an airplane pilot needs to fix an object in three dimensions.

Even with the initiatives that followed the Electra crash and others in ensuing years, bird strikes have risen sharply in recent years, as this book has made clear. The urgent need for added action was underscored by John Goglia in an interview with the *St. Petersburg Times*: "I think it's just a matter of time before we're going to have an event that will make us wish we had dealt with the problem earlier."

One thing is certain, as *Sharing the Skies* warns: "The best-laid plans of airlines, pilots, airport operators, aircraft manufacturers, investors, scientists and policy makers can easily go awry because of a few wayward birds." Yet this is most likely to happen when the aviation industry fails to coordinate its actions. As Transport Canada points out, with change an essential, vital part of aviation, the challenge is to spot safety consequences before a change is introduced. What seems a beautifully engineered solution of one problem in aviation can create a new problem elsewhere: for instance, making engines quieter unintentionally cut the escape time for birds trying their best to get out of the way of planes at airports. *Sharing the Skies* notes that systemwide safety requires—on a swift basis— the "exchange of accurate, relevant data regarding aircraft operations, airport operations, bird movements and bird strikes." The best way of doing this is by having bird strike committees at every level—local, national, and international—systematically and proactively share knowledge, experience, data, and warnings. The good news is that such committees already exist all over the globe—with sterling examples including BSC-USA and the International Bird Strike Committee.

Transport Canada drew its idea for a systemwide safety approach to prevent wildlife strikes from a best-business practice that was developed by aerospace engineering in World War II and was later adopted by many other industries in which a failure can produce a catastrophic result. It is outcome based and requires due diligence. The idea is to identify all of the complex, interwoven events that can lead to an accident. Within the system, specific responsibilities—which are closely intertwined—are assigned to various stakeholders, and as long as all parties play their roles, "the system remains intact and safety is ensured." Everyone knows who is supposed to do what, when. At GE's Aircraft Division during the Korean War, J-47 engines that had failed in combat because of imperfect polishing and balancing of turbine blades were publicly posted by serial number, with the machinist who had balanced that engine named. My father balanced many of those engines; he scrutinized the list but never saw his name on it. Accountability is a sobering thing. Systemwide safety is rooted in teamwork, and "few industries demand and promote teamwork as aggressively as aviation," since people work in what Transport Canada calls "a high consequence environment"—terrifying language indeed.

To effectively manage the risk of bird and other wildlife strikes, Transport Canada identifies three tiers, or components, that must be carefully managed; if that is done, "system safety is optimized." Those tiers offer layers of defense against damaging strikes: first, reduce exposure to bird and other wildlife hazards; second, reduce the probability of strikes; and third, reduce the severity of strikes when they occur—and they will. Each tier is like a shield held up to protect the crew and passengers of any airplane flight.

First, Reduce Exposure
For the FAA and airports to reduce exposure requires, first of all, data about the bird species causing strikes: different birds require different strategies to keep them at bay. Good wildlife science proceeds from strong data collection. Had Charles Darwin not returned from the Galápagos Islands with his log books stuffed with voluminous data, he would not be remembered today. We need accurate reporting of wildlife strikes. Why do we not have it? Transport Canada explains:

- There are no consistent worldwide standards.
- Wildlife-strike reporting is not mandatory.
- Some countries are reluctant to publish such statistics out of concern for liability and negative public perception of flight safety.
- In some parts of the world, information on serious accidents is lost for a variety of reasons, including a level of media attention lower than what we are accustomed to in the West.

To reduce exposure to wildlife hazards at airports and in our skyways, we need the strong involvement of wildlife biologists. They have become influential partners at decision-making levels at a number of vulnerable airports, like JFK and Logan, but not at all airports. Wildlife biologists should be a part of the team at every airport that gets planes in and out safely. "These experts have strenuously argued that wildlife strikes are, for the most part, not acts of God," Transport Canada notes. "Rather, such incidents are usually the results of careless management of either wildlife or habitat at and near airports, or are caused by inadequate timing, planning, and execution of flight profiles." Wildlife biologists should add their vital voice even at small airports, where they can serve on a consulting basis.

To reduce our exposure to bird strikes and to begin to build a national, systemwide safety approach, why not follow the recommendation made by John Goglia after the downing of US Airways 1549, and schedule a national summit on bird strikes? Experts from all relevant fields could gather in Washington to identify where we stand on bird strikes on aircraft, and what can be done about them. Such a summit would duly highlight bird strikes as a national transportation safety issue.

To reduce exposure to bird hazards, Transport Canada advises that, except for takeoff and landing, planes should operate at high altitudes, where birds normally do not fly. And with the skies filling up with more large birds that can fly high—like Canada geese and the turkey vulture—have come calls for planes below 10,000 feet to go no faster than 288 miles per hour. Slowing a plane's speed, we know, can reduce the severity of a bird strike.

The top method of keeping birds and planes apart is habitat control. Making our airports uninviting places for birds to feed, drink, and rest, while feeling protected from normal predators, is 80 percent of reducing exposure. That means extirpating vegetation that attracts birds, such as any plant that has fruits, nuts, or berries. In an item on its website titled "CSI for Birds: Scientists Use Forensic Techniques to Improve Airport Safety," the Smithsonian's Museum of Natural History cites techniques in development to make airport vegetation distasteful to birds:

> Researchers have found that tall fescue grass is particularly unappealing because it harbors a fungus that tastes bad to birds and gives other animals indigestion. They also test commercial products that can be sprayed onto vegetation, such as the chemical used in artificial grape flavoring, which stimulates pain receptors in birds the way hot peppers do in humans.

Airport officials should get rid of water in storm drainage ponds, which attracts shorebirds and waterfowl. An even more inventive technique, in use at some airports, is to place floating plastic balls in all ponds, to prevent birds from landing on them. Applying chemicals (with low toxicity to birds) to kill worms near runways can also help keep birds away. But a run of rainy days can wash the chemicals away, so they need to be reapplied to keep the worms from reappearing.

Is it clear now why a wildlife biologist is needed at every airport?

The issues and problems can be complex and will vary with the species of wildlife making appearances at each airport.

Other actions include ridding airports promptly of bird carcasses, which can attract vultures. Bird carcasses end up on a runway following collisions with aircraft. A collision can go unnoticed by the pilot when it caused no damage to the plane—it just killed the bird.

Clearing airports of trees, ledges, and other sites that provide perches for birds is important. Keeping hangar doors shut when they do not need to be open can keep a bird from flying in and roosting inside.

Reducing wildlife hazards at airports does not end with aggressive habitat control by airport officials. Municipal leaders need to keep landfills, other waste-disposal sites, and junkyards from being located close to the airport; restaurants and farms near airports need to avoid practices that attract birds. All of these matters need to be closely monitored: one change by one stakeholder in the tightly linked world of aviation, as Transport Canada points out, can throw off risk management actions carried out by others.

Second, Reduce Probability
What should we do when, even after due diligence in reducing exposure, birds show up near airplanes, either at airports or in the skyways? We move to the second tier of protection: we reduce the probability of a strike. The tools for use here are many, and fortunately increasing. Transport Canada outlines how to deal with the hazard's proximity through detection, deterrence, and avoidance.

Airport staff should systematically patrol airport environs, looking for signs of birds and other wildlife hazards. Other staff should scan runways and apron areas with binoculars. When birds or mammals are spotted, teams should be dispatched to deal with the hazard by appropriate means, which will depend on the wildlife species. Interestingly, the first means used to disperse birds is an ancient one. make noise, and plenty of it. Katherine Tweed, in a sidebar to Bruce Barcott's *Audubon* article on bird dispersal tactics at airports, quotes John Ostrom, the chair of BSC-USA, on one cheap method: "the human being out there hooting and hollering." Ostrom notes: "If you want to move birds, 'shoo, shoo, shoo' still works."

Other prime tools used to frighten off birds are: barking dogs, propane cannons, firearms, and flares. Tweed mentions "distress-cry generators which broadcast digitally recorded birds sounds." Other devices to scare off birds include small, radio-controlled airplanes. Experiments with swooping red-tailed hawks are underway at some airports to frighten off smaller birds, but there is a danger that the hawk itself could become a bird hazard, sucked into a jet engine. Trained falcons, more controllable than red-tailed hawks, are, as mentioned above, being tried at JFK—not to hunt other birds, but just to fly around for a while, since their presence instantly scares off gulls and other birds. The truth is, as Tweed observes, that "no single technique will always keep birds out of flight paths, so airports use a variety of strategies." Indeed, the repertoire of scare tactics actually needs to vary; otherwise birds will become habituated to the methods and ignore them.

An example of the periodic need to shift tactics occurred in 2007 in Afghanistan, at the U.S. Air Force base at Bagram. The base had been using "bangers and screamers," rockets fired at birds that make a noise like a siren, followed by a loud bang. That was frightening to the birds at first, but the method began to lose its power: bird strikes at Bagram doubled from one year to the next. The Defense Department then put out bids for trained falconers to come to Afghanistan to clear away birds from the air base. A systemwide safe approach must always include being alert to changes—in aviation, in nature, and in the best method to be employed at any one time.

By far the most novel method of bird dispersal is being used at the Minneapolis-St. Paul International Airport. As Tweed reports, officials fire paintball guns "into and just outside of flocks that don't budge when pyrotechnics are set off."

Bird capture and relocation is a tactic used quite successfully in certain circumstances. On February 2, 2009, *The Boston Globe* ran an article by Brian Ballou on the winter return to Logan of majestic, wide-eyed snowy owls. They arrive in winter and take up temporary residence, before returning to the Arctic at the season's end. In recent years, the owl population has increased, and now the birds pose a danger to air traffic. Ballou writes: "Logan's problem is Norm Smith's passion. Smith, an owl specialist with the Massachusetts Audubon Society, has been helping the airport remove the owls since 1981. So far, he figures he has trapped and removed 360. This winter, he has removed 21." Smith tags and then removes the owls to choice locales outside the city, often to beautiful Plum Island, north of Boston.

David Ishira, the director of airport aviation operations, commented to Ballou: "We don't want Logan to become a wildlife habitat. . . . We know we can't eliminate the wildlife here, but our goal is to manage it." Ishira said of Norm Smith: "When there's an opportunity to team up with him, it's a win-win situation." This is systemwide safety at its tightly coordinated best.

Pilots play a vital role in reducing the probability of a bird strike. They can often initiate early action to avoid collisions with birds once they see them, and then communicate critical bird hazard information— size, numbers, and species of birds—to officials on the ground, who relay it in turn to others both on the ground and in the air. By using bright landing lights, pilots can raise the probability that wildlife will see the aircraft and get well out of the way. Recent evidence suggests that pulsing landing lights give still earlier warning to wildlife of a plane's approach.

High technology bird dispersal devices are always being explored; "audible radar" is one mentioned by Transport Canada. Scientists believe that some wildlife can hear microwaves, which seem dangerous and prompt the animal to move away. Microwave-emitting radar systems could be mounted on aircraft and project microwaves one mile ahead, to give early warning to birds.

Most encouraging of all the high-technology dispersal devices is low-power laser light, which disperses birds in a plane's flight path without causing any damage to the birds' eyes. However, early research suggests that the lasers work on some species but not others—on Canada geese, but not on brown-headed cowbirds or European starlings— illustrating once again that risk management is species specific.

Where possible, pilots should follow routes that avoid high concentrations of birds. Much is happening in terms of the latest high-tech resources that can aid pilots to do this, as will be discussed below.

The success of all tactics—of the entire systemwide safety approach—turns on timely, accurate communication to avoid bird and other wildlife strikes. Everyone in the aviation industry and those connected to it must act systematically and proactively to save planes and lives.

Third, Reduce the Severity

If humans do everything they can to reduce exposure to bird strike (the strategic front) and to reduce the probability of a strike (the tactical front), yet birds actually manage to strike an aircraft, what can be done to reduce the severity of that strike?

Aircraft manufacturers need to develop windscreens, airplane frames, and jet engines far better able to withstand bird strikes, especially those from a large bird or from more than one bird, with the machine-gun effect of multiple strikes—or, of course, from multiple strikes by large birds. Recall Sullenberger's stomach-sinking comment: "Loud thumps . . . like the worst thunderstorm I'd ever heard growing up in Texas." Some manufacturers are working on windscreens and other aircraft parts that can deflect birds.

Jetliner pilots should not be required to be expert glider pilots like Sullenberger. Redundancy in aircraft engines—adding a third and fourth engine—should be included with other changes in design that can boost the chance of a filled jetliner's surviving a direct hit by a flock of big birds, with some engine power left to land safely on an airfield, not a river.

It may be useful to recall here just how full of birds the skies are. From Europe and Asia to Africa and back again, 280 species of birds—including pelicans, storks, honey buzzards, cranes, and lesser flamingos—migrate over the tiny nation of Israel alone on a route so ancient that Abraham, Isaac, Sarah, Rachel, and other figures from the Old Testament almost certainly marveled at them. And the birds are so common today that the Israeli Air Force created posters to warn pilots—"Take care—we share the air"—as recounted in a stunningly beautiful book by Carole Garbuny Vogel and the Israeli ornithologist, Yossi Leshem, *The Man Who Flies with Birds*. Leshem's work has saved the lives of many Israeli pilots who must take off daily and fly fast at low altitudes in a country which can be traversed in twelve minutes, and whose skies are often filled with many millions of large birds. As the authors point out: "During the 1960s and 1970s, the Israeli Air Force was losing more planes to birds than to hostile fire." The situation took a turn for the worse in 1982, when Israel gave the Sinai back to Egypt; the Sinai is an area three times larger than Israel today, which is a bit smaller than New Jersey. By vigilant, passionate tracking of migratory patterns, aided by a legion of volunteers, Leshem was able to give crucial flight planning advice to the Israeli Air Force and reduce significantly the number of plane-bird collisions. The Israeli Air Force now routinely integrates migratory data into flight route planning and flight scheduling, which has led to a dramatic reduction in fatalities and losses of costly aircraft.

Airline training programs for pilots worldwide need to give major attention to dealing with wildlife strikes competently and confidently, requiring pilots to maintain their proficiency in emergency procedures. Pilots should also be taught to use the latest technology to plan prudent, well-timed flight routes that, wherever possible, avoid exposure to bird hazards in the first place. At the moment, military pilots would be far more successful than commercial pilots in doing so. Because of far more rigid schedules and flight routes, the commercial pilot is likelier to have to take off with "the bell-beat of their wings above my head." That quotation, the epigraph of this book, is from Yeats's "The Wild Swans at Coole." By the way, the average male mute swan weighs twenty-six pounds and tops both the list of the fourteen largest North American birds by weight and the list of large birds with the highest rates of population increases. It is one of the heaviest flying birds in the world—not a good bird to be ingested into the engines of your twinjet.

An Alphabet Soup of Protection: BAM, AHAS, NEXRAD

In the early 1980s, the U.S. Air Force began to develop a Bird Avoidance Model (BAM) to help flight crews avoid dangerous bird strikes. The concept was visionary: to reach back to rich historical data about bird migrations and breeding habits and link the information to ever-improving computer technology able to riff through vast amounts of data and offer up timely advisories "to protect human lives, wildlife, and equipment during air operations throughout the coterminous United States and Alaska," as the BAM website states. In developing BAM, the Air Force focused on the sixty most hazardous bird species in the United States, taking its data from the Audubon Society's famed Christmas bird count; the Breeding Bird Survey, a joint effort of the U.S. Geological Survey's Patuxent Wildlife Research Center and the Canadian Wildlife Service's National Wildlife Research Centre; bird refuge arrival and departure dates; and other reliable sources.

With BAM, potential bird density is overlaid onto a standard map, and each square kilometer is assigned a bird-strike risk value. There are three predicted risk categories to encapsulate conditions for busy flight crews and flight planners: low, moderate, and severe, as measured by bird mass per square kilometer, with risk levels rising logarithmically across categories. Thus, a moderate zone is 57–708 times riskier than a low zone, and a severe zone is a terrorizing 2,503–38,647 times riskier. The last category means if you're not carrying out an essential mission, don't fly. As Transport Canada points out, BAM "allows users to obtain bird-hazard information according to geographic locations, time of year, time of day, and selected routes. By comparing the relative risk of different flight plans, users are able to select the safest times and locations in which to fly."

The U.S. Air Force rightfully warns that since "birds are dynamic creatures whose migratory behavior is initiated by weather events in any given year, the model cannot be said to predict the exact movement of bird species through space and time beyond the biweekly time frame." BAM models give risks for dawn, day, dusk, and night, for each of twenty-six annual two-week periods. These models are useful up to twenty-four hours before a flight. To obtain real-time data for the twenty-four hours before they take off, pilots need to consult the Avian Hazard Advisory Systems (AHAS) for risk prediction of bird movements. AHAS pulls valuable Doppler information about bird activity from next-generation weather radar (NEXRAD). AHAS updates bird strike risk in cycles of twenty to twenty-five minutes.

The hope is that the airport-based avian radar systems discussed earlier eventually might be integrated with the historical BAM and the real-time Doppler-driven dynamic maps of AHAS to provide fluid, integrated, accurate "bird weather" forecasts. Then, when a pilot climbs into the plane and throughout the flight, he or she will know everything about where birds are concentrated. However, we have a long way to go. As Russ DeFusco, a top expert on bird strikes, says in Bruce Barcott's article: "Where we are with birds today is something like where we were with weather forecasting 50 years ago."

In the documentary film titled *Birds*, the narrator says: "As long as birds reach for the heavens, our imagination will soar along with them." Let's put that soaring imagination to work to find a way to share the skies, safely and fairly, with the birds that first inspired us to do what John Magee described so eloquently in his poem: "I have slipped the surly bonds of Earth . . . and touched the face of God."

7 The Making of a Patron Saint

Passion is our ground, our island—do others exist?
—Eudora Welty, "Circe"

When you first meet him, John Goglia doesn't strike you as a saint. He's built like a middle linebacker and has a handshake that would make a polar bear wince. He speaks with a pitch-perfect Boston accent, apt for the recent epoch of Boston noir films. Indeed, if he had been thirty years younger, Goglia could have replaced Matt Damon in *Good Will Hunting*, not only for his accent, but for a portrayal of someone both tough and curious, a compulsive reader, and a closet genius from a working-class neighborhood. In the film, Damon's character, Will Hunting, shoots down a stuffed-shirt Harvard graduate student in a Cambridge bar by having hopelessly outread the fellow in his own arcane field. That's Goglia: tough, well-read, and not afraid to mix it up, especially on behalf of somebody else.

Saints do not come only in flowing robes as painted by the masters. They also come in the work clothes of a skilled aviation mechanic with a valid library card, an unerring sense of right and wrong, and a heart as big as the Ritz. Goglia well deserves the epithet pinned on him by the media: the patron saint of travel safety.

The National Air Disaster Alliance gave Goglia its Aviation Safety Award for his compassionate concern for the families of crash victims; the International Symposium on Aviation Emergencies bestowed on him its first Aviation Safety Advocate of the Year Award; the Professional Aviation Maintenance Association honored him with its Joe Chase Award for his outstanding work in improving the knowledge, safety, and dignity of aircraft technicians. Goglia served on the National Transportation Safety Board (NTSB) from 1995 until 2004, and for twenty years before that took part in many aviation crash investigations, some involving horrific loss of life. He has always been dedicated to finding the truth, telling it, and preventing future accidents. When Goglia stepped down from the NTSB, David A. Lombardo, writing in Aviation International News (AIN) online quoted an attendee at a ceremony honoring Goglia: "The man's like a pit bull. He flat out refuses to give up, and when he figures out what happened he flat out refuses to be politically correct. He'll just blurt it out in front of God and television cameras with absolutely no concern for his own career or what cages he's rattling." In a 2004 *St. Petersburg Times* profile on Goglia, Bill Adair, the newspaper's Washington bureau chief, offered this take on Goglia from Jack Kreckie, an airport fire-rescue official: "He knows where all the skeletons are buried and he's not afraid to kick the doors down and reveal them. . . . This guy operates from his heart."

People don't always agree with Goglia, but everyone seems to trust him. When he was appointed to the NTSB, as Lombardo notes, it was with the support of the Air Transport Association, the principal trade association of U.S. airline companies. A representative of the association stated: "It's not that we're in love with Goglia but we know he doesn't blow in the wind like a willow."

Never shy, always forthright, he told somebody who challenged him at an NTSB hearing: "The President put me here for my opinion. It may not be right, but it's my opinion. If it's not right, convince me where I am wrong, and I'll change. But otherwise I stand by my opinion." On a personal level, says Lombardo: "Goglia is a handshake guy. . . . He'd sooner die than break his word." The respect he has earned all around serves him well; the article on Goglia in *Magis* noted that the head safety official for Korean Airlines flew in for Goglia's NTSB retirement party and said of Goglia: "He has the ability to pull together people who otherwise would probably never come and sit at the table together." Goglia's career followed a dramatically unorthodox arc, from line aviation mechanic to one of the nation's top transportation crash experts. He was often the person reporters contacted when they wanted a quick, reliable quote and the unvarnished truth.

To set the National Transportation and Safety Board in context, it was established in 1967 as an independent agency responsible for civil transportation accident investigations, taking over that role from the Civil Aeronautics Board, which had investigated the Boston Electra crash. The NTSB initially had close ties to the Department of Transportation, but those were cut in 1975 to ensure that the findings of the NTSB would be truly independent. As an example of its independence, Goglia reports that in his nine years on the board, no member ever received a call from the White House—the source of NTSB appointments. The board has five members, each appointed by the president. One key test of such an agency's independence is who gets blamed; if every time it is a dead pilot who is considered responsible for the crash—or most times, with occasionally a living pilot blamed—as once was the case, then something is amiss. Goglia commented about that past behavior: "Yeah, sometimes the pilot screwed up at the end, but what were the events leading up to the crash? Those would never get the sunshine that they needed."

When Goglia was offered a place on the NTSB, he hesitated since he would need to cut all ties to USAir, his longtime employer—and that meant giving up $3,500 a month in retirement pay and his health benefits. When Goglia told the USAir vice-president for maintenance that he might not take the position, the vice-president said, "You have to take it! No one from our field has ever made it up to the NTSB." "Our field" referred to the 140,000 aviation mechanics in the United States at the time. In the end, Goglia sacrificed pay and benefits, as he says, "for the opportunity to make a difference." For him, making a difference means making the daily travel of hundreds of millions of Americans safer—by car, boat, bus, train, or plane.

"Virtually all accidents are preventable," Goglia believes, but he quickly adds: "There is nothing new in accidents," only our persistent failure to implement best practices systemwide. In the 2005 article about him in *Magis*, Goglia is quoted as saying: "The NTSB only recommends changes, and these changes sometimes take forever to get implemented, if they get implemented." He added, "So really, the best way is to get out there on the front end and use that same process to prevent accidents in the first place."

In reflecting back on his NTSB service, he observed that "virtually every one of them [the accidents] was preventable, if we had just applied what already we knew." "John Goglia Is a Man on a Mission," read the article's title, and that mission is to prevent accidents and, should they occur, for us to be far better prepared to deal with them.

Goglia never forgets that when you travel, loved ones at home are praying for your safe return. That's one of the reasons why he cries openly when he talks to the families of people killed in transportation crashes; why he fights so hard to find the truth of what caused a crash when others would just as soon hide inconvenient facts; and why he believes so strongly in treating families with sensitivity and compassion—which includes keeping them truthfully and regularly informed about the progress of the accident investigation.

Time in the Water

All stories have beginnings, and Goglia's begins with time in the water on October 4, 1960, between the setting of a crimson sun and the rising of a blood-red moon. He was sixteen years old.

There is no question that the direction Goglia's life took toward travel safety was partly caused by his time in Winthrop Harbor, scuba tank on his back, slipping below the blood-streaked water and resurfacing with body parts in his hands. When he entered the water an hour after the crash of the Boston Electra, it was to do not rescue work but recovery work: to find corpses and parts of corpses. The following text includes quotes from Goglia about that experience and his early journey toward his vocation. (These come from my lengthy interviews with him in 2007, 2008, and 2009.)

> I believe that everything in life leaves a mark on you, and a mark was left on me that night. It was the first time I ever held pieces of people in my hand. You don't forget that. Fortunately, I was young and invincible. I was already in love with aviation but the blood-and-guts aspect,

the wanting to make a difference, absolutely was affected by that experience. There were sights and scenes that day that I will never forget.

How did Goglia become a trained diver at sixteen, which led to his being in the water that day? Oddly, it came from his being a self-confessed compulsive reader from a young age—a child who flagged down the Boston Public Library's bookmobile as it rolled through the streets of his native East Boston.

I learned to dive by way of Jim Walton of Newburyport. I got to know Jim because he was a diver. Later he became a famous commercial diver; his name [was] always in the newspapers. But back then you couldn't make a living as a diver, so he drove the public library bookmobile, which came to East Boston. So, every time the bookmobile was in the neighborhood, I was in it, and he was pumping up the diving stuff. In 1958, when I was fourteen, he invited me up to his place on Plum Island; and I went up for a few days and learned to water ski. My parents had to drive me up and pick me up. That's when he got me hooked on the diving. Some time over the winter, when it wasn't popular to do so, when you put tanks on people's backs and put them in a pool or the ocean to teach them to dive—he made me go through a rigorous program; he made me sit down and study the charts, learn what the bends is, and so on. Before I ever went into the water, he had pounded that stuff into my head. By 1959 I had started to dive and by 1960 I had diving gear—though never new gear. But always there was a steady stream of people who thought they wanted to dive, and then they would come back through later and try to get rid of the gear. And, since I was supporting Jim's efforts at his diving school up in Newburyport, helping people to get the gear on, he gave me some dive equipment. For some of it I had to scrape money together and buy it. Jim helped to train the first State Police and City of Boston dive teams. In any event, right after the plane crash, I got a call from him, asking, "Do you have your gear?" I did and by chance the tanks were charged. Minutes later Walton came by in a police cruiser to pick me up.

Goglia paused, his eyes twinkling, and added: "It was the only time I ever rode in a police cruiser *voluntarily*."

Hooked on Aviation

As mentioned earlier and fully recounted in Adair's profile of Goglia in the *St. Petersburg Times,* when Goglia was a teenager, he rode his bicycle all around Logan Airport—which was close to his home—making friends with the mechanics, who let him climb all over and inside the DC-3s and DC-6s. His mother, an employee of American Airlines, was well aware of the high salaries earned by commercial airline pilots, so she encouraged him to think about becoming a pilot. In 1959, he began flying lessons in Marlborough, Massachusetts, and soon soloed. Indeed, he flew freely on his own in and out of Marlborough airport "on my student pilot ticket," never even seeing an FAA inspector. The FAA had been established the year before, and its employees were busy getting the agency up and running. Flying was not Goglia's true love, and he gave it up after a couple of years.

By the time of his graduation from Boston English High School in 1962, he had decided he wanted to become a state trooper. On his mother's side, the Irish side, he had "tons of relatives who were firefighters," who were role models for him of people who serve and protect the public. The ethic of firefighters and police to race toward problems and danger as others flee, fully evident on 9/11, stayed with Goglia. It would come to characterize his work investigating some of the major transportation accidents of his time. He never backpedaled away from problems; instead, just like the firefighters in his family, he always raced toward them.

Goglia could not become a state trooper after graduating from high school: you had to be twenty-one, and he was barely eighteen. So he was intrigued when he saw an advertisement for East Coast Aerotech's eighteen-month intensive program to learn to be an FAA-licensed A&P mechanic, like the men he had befriended as a boy at Logan ("A&P" refers to airframe and power plant). As described by the Aviation Institute of Maintenance, "an A&P license allows mechanics to work on the airframe and power plant of an aircraft without supervision and allows the mechanic in some situations to return an aircraft to flight status."

Although Goglia's mother would have preferred him to become a pilot, she knew that aviation mechanics earned good salaries, and so she supported his decision to enroll in the East Coast Aerotech program, in Bedford, Massachusetts. He graduated in 1963. Later he would earn bachelor's and master's degrees in business from Devonshire College, become an adjunct professor of aviation science at Saint Louis University, receive two honorary degrees from aviation colleges, and be asked to deliver the commencement address on one of those occasions (not surprisingly, the topic he chose was ethics).

The Route to Accident Investigation
After graduating from East Coast Aerotech, Goglia went to work as an aviation mechanic for United Airlines in New York, mostly at JFK. But before long, United began layoffs in New York. Low in seniority, Goglia could continue to work for United only if he went to one of the Washington area airports. He secured a post in Baltimore. In 1965, he married Patricia Guarino, also of East Boston. Patricia had lived around the corner from John, but they had not known each other as children, mostly because John went to Catholic school and Patricia to public school.

After John had been in Baltimore for a couple of years, United began layoffs there as well. To stay with United, he would need to move to San Francisco, but Patricia was eager to return to Boston to be close to family. Goglia learned from a friend that Allegheny was hiring in Boston; he applied, and, with his several years of experience, Allegheny grabbed him up.

The move to Allegheny made all the difference in Goglia's career. Where United Airlines tended to pigeonhole employees by job title, Allegheny was open; a talented employee with initiative could take on new tasks that often fell outside the job description. Allegheny was a regional airline, but it was clearly on the move—its business model was to grow by affiliating with other regional airlines and merging with still others. It was on a fast track to becoming a national airline. In 1979 Allegheny changed its name to USAir to shed its regional image and expand west and south.

When Goglia arrived at Allegheny, the airline's small size fed its naturally open culture; with limited manpower, why not creatively use the talent at hand to further the company's objectives? Goglia was one of only ten Allegheny mechanics in Boston. At Allegheny, he would have scope to use his full powers.

With the Airline Deregulation Act of 1978, Allegheny was freer to pursue its goal of becoming a national airline. After rebranding itself a couple of times, it became USAirways, the nation's fifth largest airline and the employer of Captain Sullenberger.

Goglia usually worked from 11:00 p.m. until 7:00 a.m. "As long as you gave them planes that took off right on time in the morning and flew all day long, they didn't bother you with busy work," he recalls. So, when he had time on his hands, which he often did, he would turn to the reading material he had inevitably brought with him when he punched in. To this day he remains a world-class reader: compulsively inquisitive. He says: "Give me a few minutes and I reach for one of my books. If it wasn't for the Discovery Channel, National Geo, and those channels, I wouldn't even need a television."

Since this characteristic helps to explain Goglia's ascent to nationally known crash expert, it is worth pondering his recent reading. Ever since he learned through reading that the makings of Portland cement were found on the moon, he has been reading about concrete. After his discovery, he concluded that meant if water were also found on the moon, space ships could be built there of concrete. If this sounds bizarre, it is not. First of all, a few months after he began this reading jag, and a couple of days before the writing of this chapter, NASA announced that there certainly is water on the moon, in the form of ice. Yes, but who would want to build space ships out of concrete? Concrete is resistant to penetration by radiation, and as Goglia points out, the earth is surrounded by belts of radiation that are lethal to spaceships and human travelers: long-range space travel is precluded unless we find a way to penetrate the radiation belts safely.

Some design engineers believe the next generation of aerospace material will be concrete—not your grandfather's concrete, but concrete blended with other ingredients to make it so light it can float, and so flexible it won't break. And there are engineers now testing such lightweight concrete in the form of swift-moving canoes. Why does concrete have the properties it does? Goglia is probably using his library card to find out.

In any event, in his early years at Allegheny, Goglia served as lead mechanic on the midnight shift and as shop steward. His tilt toward safety issues at work began in 1972, when the local of the International Association of Machinists (IAM) began a ground safety program to reduce injuries on the job, something much appreciated by management since those injuries can prove costly to a company. Goglia describes the work as "OSHA work before there was an OSHA." He just took on the task as an added assignment. Not long afterward, the union began to look at matters of flight safety—the safety of the aircraft. Goglia was involved with both ground safety and flight safety until the work became too great for one person to deal with both. He picked flight safety, leaving ground safety to someone else.

All the while Allegheny was growing. In 1974, after its merger with Mohawk Airlines, there was a runway overrun accident in Rochester, New York. With his growing familiarity with safety issues, Goglia was sent to Rochester with the Allegheny team to work on the NTSB accident investigation. In the evenings, back at the hotel, his curiosity and reading compulsion clicked on. He began diving into the whole process of how the NTSB investigated crashes, and studying past investigations of aviation accidents. When I asked him, "Can you recommend any books on aviation accidents," his reply was: "What are you looking for? I own them all." In effect, he had created for himself an independent graduate degree program in NTSB proceedings and aviation accident investigation. He built a chrysalis, crawled in, and emerged a national crash expert. It is impossible here not to hark back to *Good Will Hunting* and Will's comment after deflating the pompous Harvard grad student, which he had done only because the other man had embarrassed Will's friend to impress a couple of female Harvard students: "You dropped a hundred and fifty grand on an education you could have gotten for a dollar fifty in late charges at the public library."

Go-Go Goglia
Goglia had mastered the work of an aviation mechanic and had become bored; the true challenge, he felt, was keeping Allegheny's aging and motley fleet of planes fit and flying on a daily basis. Early in his

work life he had gained the nickname Go-Go Goglia, after a manager who stuttered referred to him that way. But the moniker stuck because it seemed apt: he needed either to be reading and learning or tackling some new problem, using his mechanic's attitude—find it, fix it, move on to the next problem. He was to bring that aggressive approach to accident investigation.

As Goglia became increasingly savvy about how the NTSB operated, he became increasingly valuable both to the union and to management. Having been a shop steward, he was trusted by labor; as someone smart, increasingly knowledgeable about a range of aviation issues, and a man of his word, he was trusted by management. And he never stopped at book learning; he was always willing to take on new tasks to learn more. He came to see that, with large companies and large unions, "while we often think of labor and management in a logjam on every issue, that's not true. On a whole range of issues they have mutual interests."

Bill Sutherland, a district manager for IAM, was a mentor to Goglia. Goglia remembers Sutherland telling him, when he was still a young man: "You're only as good as your word. When you commit to something, be committed even if it hurts. Stand tall. Tell the truth."

"That advice has served me well in life," Goglia says. After Allegheny's name change to USAir, the airline continued to absorb other regional airlines—with John sent out into the field by management to help smooth the way. The company was giving him more and more responsibility, unrelated to his job title: aviation mechanic. In 1985 he was sent for a whole year to San Diego to work on USAir's merger with Pacific Southwest Airlines; shortly after he returned, he was sent to Winston-Salem to work on a merger with Piedmont Airlines. Those two mergers allowed USAir to grow dramatically.

On the accident investigation front, "lo and behold, I had become the guy in the union with all the information, all the expertise, the one who knew the most about accident investigation." And that meant the entire IAM union, a million strong at the time, with more than 100,000 members in aviation alone. By the mid-1980s, Go-Go-Goglia was the go-to-guy on aviation accidents—not only for accidents affecting USAir, but those involving any airline with an IAM local.

Goglia observes: "As the national union matured on accident investigations, they wanted to spread knowledge of the NTSB process to other union locals," so that the machinists' union could be an active, effective participant in federal investigations as the pilots' association had long been—dating back to the days of the CAB, even before the Boston Electra crash. Goglia led the way on union training about the NTSB, with the union paying USAir for Goglia's lost time. When an aviation accident happened, Goglia inevitably was one of the first people called, offering advice to the team working on the accident, sometimes even back at the hotel helping the team to prepare for NTSB hearings. USAir developed a reputation for having the best accident investigation team on the mechanics' side, because it had Goglia at its core. IAM wanted all union locals to have the benefit of Goglia's knowledge, no matter which particular airlines the mechanics worked for.

How did Goglia's increased responsibility, both with the company and the union, affect him personally? He says: "It increased my desire to stop turning wrenches."

Rising National Profile

All of Goglia's skills would be called upon when USAir suffered five crashes in five years, the fifth near Pittsburgh in September 1994, with the fourth just three months earlier. It was an emotionally crushing time for all of USAir's employees. As Goglia told *Magis*: "We hadn't even been able to unload the emotional baggage from the accident in July when we got hit with the September accident." In a dramatic moment that September, captured by Adair in his *St. Petersburg Times* profile, a Pittsburgh hotel room was filled with pilots and mechanics investigating the crash of yet another USAir plane, and nearly everyone was crying; "big tears rolled down [Goglia's] cheeks." Choking back his tears, Goglia hugged the leader of the pilots union and said: "Our goal is to make sure no one has to go through this again."

The fifth crash was that of USAir Flight 427 near Pittsburgh, a crash Adair would write of at length in *The Mystery of Flight 427: Inside a Crash Investigation*. The Boeing 737 was destroyed, with all 132 people on board killed. The pilots had suddenly lost all ability to control the airplane, and it had struck the ground on the nearly vertical, as in the

Boston Electra crash, with the same pile-up of passengers in the front of the aircraft.

A doctor assigned to debrief USAir staff in Pittsburgh, who debriefed Goglia twice, told him to cry out his grief. "You have to unload it somehow, and I unloaded it just by crying," he told *Magis*. The crying is genuine and appreciated by families of those killed in aviation crashes as a sign of empathy—something they don't often perceive from others in a profession that is, in Adair's phrase, "dominated by macho guys who hide their emotions."

Before Goglia's appointment to the NTSB, much of his work centered on high-profile investigations of aviation crashes, but he was also respected for his extensive behind-the-scenes work. A prime example was Goglia's deep involvement in the FAA's review of all federal aviation regulations pertaining to flight safety and maintenance. That review was triggered in the early 1990s by Transportation Secretary Federico Peña's "Zero Accident Initiative." David Lombardo reports that the Department of Transportation wanted industry participation, and both USAir and IAM supported Goglia's involvement. He sat on twenty-two committees and chaired three. As he told Lombardo: "That's when I got my reputation about calling it the way I see it. I would alternately anger the union and then the company." Lombardo astutely observed: "The reputation would lead to an unforeseen opportunity."

The NTSB Years

Lombardo described how Goglia became a Clinton appointee to the NTSB. Goglia said: "I was doing everything else for the company you can imagine except working as a mechanic." Since he had so much accident investigation experience, when a position opened on the NTSB he filed an application. A week later he was in Washington and his pager went off; it was his wife, and when he called home from a pay phone, he learned that the White House was trying to reach him. From the same phone booth he called the woman who had spoken to his wife, and he learned that someone at the White House would like to see him. "How soon can you come to Washington?" the woman asked. Goglia replied, "Is five minutes too long? I am at 17th and

H Street, looking at the White House right now." The woman laughed and arranged an appointment for him later that afternoon with the head of personnel at the White House, Elizabeth Montoya. Based on that conversation, Goglia realized that the interest in him was genuine, not just a courtesy matter, and he began to line up supporters. Although appointment to the NTSB is normally a political appointment, the Clinton administration liked Goglia precisely because he was nonpolitical; voter rolls in Massachusetts listed him as "unenrolled"—neither Democrat, Republican, nor independent. With President Clinton in trouble because of the Monica Lewinsky scandal, the White House wanted someone nonpolitical. Goglia fit the bill, right down to his reputation for calling things as he sees them. And he was an unquestioned aviation accident expert.

The high-charging Go-Go-Goglia work ethic was evident when he joined the NTSB. He often worked late into the night, nothing new to someone who had been a midnight shift mechanic. Adair reported that Goglia would call people at all hours, citing the occasion when he "called a Pratt & Whitney safety official at 2 A.M. to discuss birds. When he calls, he skips the formality of identifying himself. He just says, 'Whattya you doin? Did I wake you up?'"

On the board, Goglia showed his usual blunt, open, politically incorrect self, both publicly and privately. "I have never been politically correct my whole life," he's quick to say.

"His impulsive style ruffled feathers in the cautious culture of the NTSB," Adair wrote, quoting former NTSB managing director Peter Goelz: "Upper management [of the NTSB] always thought that he could be a pain in the a––. But the tin kickers loved him. They knew he was one of them." With no regard for diplomacy, Goglia "once chastised a federal official for withholding a safety report by saying, 'This really smells.'"

Since the NTSB could not make changes itself, but only recommend them, the board often took strong positions with the FAA and the Railroad Administration so that in the final give-and-take, the end result would still lead to some advancement in travel safety.

When President Clinton appointed Goglia to the NTSB, Goglia fit no prior model. The NTSB appointments are included in the *Plum*

Book, which lists 7,000 federal jobs—some important, some not—to which a president can appoint people, most of which are used to reward somebody for political reasons. Ambassadorships are the classic example.

The NTSB, Goglia observes, is a perfect perch for lawyers, who often come to the board without knowing much about investigating accidents. Those who are appointed are supposed to be at least technically qualified, a requirement easy enough to meet in the gap between a president's election and inauguration. As Goglia told David Lombardo: "You go out to Arizona, enroll in a flight-training course and within a few weeks time you're a pilot. Presto, you qualify to be an NTSB board member." As a lawyer, when you leave the board, "you've got a guaranteed law practice." Goglia was an unusual board member because he was a technical expert.

The *Magis* article about Goglia said that "no one has shed more tears on national television than him—except maybe Tammy Faye"— the reference is to televangelist Jim Bakker's wife, Tammy Faye Bakker, famed for crying rivers of liquefied mascara. A lot of Goglia's crying while on the NTSB was with surviving relatives of crash victims, who came to love him as their protector and informant. He fought for the truth, told them the truth, and was not afraid to cry in front of them.

Let us look at a few examples.

The Fox River Grove Bus Crash

On October 25, 1995, seven students from Cary Grove High School in Cary, Illinois, were killed in Fox River Grove, Illinois, when a train slammed into their school bus. The bus was stopped at a red light, the back of the bus jutting over the tracks. There were more than two dozen students on the bus. The train had begun slowing, but too late; it was traveling at sixty miles per hour when it struck the bus.

Goglia was a member of the on-scene NTSB investigation team. When he arrived on the crash site, he did what he always did at an accident scene—he stood outside the police tape and, anonymously, listened to what ordinary people had to say about the accident. He always did this before talking to local authorities who might have some reason to shade the truth. As he eavesdropped, he heard people say that sometimes the railroad crossing equipment failed. So he had the entire railroad crossing gear packed up and shipped off to NTSB experts, who ran it through hundreds of cycles until the sporadic failure occurred. The NTSB ultimately determined that the Illinois Department of Transportation did not properly recognize that the rail crossings were poorly designed and criticized school districts for not spotting the danger. Goglia told *Magis:* "My actions there caused a little ripple in Washington because I was aggressive in going after it. I have a job to do, and I'm going to do it." After the NTSB's finding, multimillion-dollar lawsuits were filed.

Some years after the Fox River Grove crash, Goglia was giving a talk at Parks College at Saint Louis University, where he was an adjunct professor of aviation science. After the talk, one of the students at the college, who was from Fox River Grove, hung around after everyone else had left to thank Goglia personally for all he had done in the investigation. "That got to me," Goglia told *Magis.*

The ValuJet Flight 592 Crash

In Goglia's two terms on the NTSB, one of the many ghastly aviation crashes he investigated was the fiery ValuJet crash in the Florida Everglades on May 11, 1996. A ValuJet DC-9 en route from Miami to Atlanta crashed soon after takeoff in the Everglades, killing all 110 people on board. Goglia recalls hearing on the plane's recorder the screams of passengers who were "cooking in the back." He chaired the NTSB's public hearings.

As he told *Magis:* "ValuJet was a big deal. That was where the staff was going in one direction and I disagreed. I took them on in public and got the report changed." The NTSB found that the fire that had caused the crash had begun in the plane's cargo hold, fueled by dozens of oxygen-generating canisters that had been mislabeled. The report led to changes both at the FAA and in the aviation industry; new rules mandated that all commercial jets have fire detection and suspension equipment in cargo compartments. The NTSB concluded the crash had been avoidable, the result of failures by the airline, its maintenance contractor, and the FAA.

During the NTSB investigation, Goglia vowed to the families of the crash's victims that they would know the truth of what caused the crash: "If there is any cover-up, here's the way you'll know: My seat on the Board will be empty." He would give the identical assurance to the families of the victims of the crash of TWA Flight 800, discussed below, which happened just a few months after the ValuJet crash.

Goglia said: "It was my attitude on the Board, 'The facts are the facts. I didn't make the mess. It helps to get the truth out.'" He has also commented: "When you tell the truth, people might be ticked at you, but there's nothing they can do about it."

The TWA Flight 800 Crash
On July 17, 1996, a Boeing 747 took off from JFK bound for Paris; it exploded shortly after takeoff and crashed in the Atlantic Ocean off Long Island. All 230 people on board were killed. The probable cause of the crash, as determined by the NTSB, was an explosion of the center wing fuel tank, most likely the result of faulty wiring. Theories abounded, including a bomb on board or an external missile fired at the aircraft; no evidence of a bomb or a missile was ever found. The NTSB focused on several safety issues as probable cause, as Goglia told *Magis*: fuel tank flammability, numerous potential ignition sources, and aging aircraft wiring. He said: "We knew there had been an explosion inside the fuel tank, but it was a monumental task to prove to people who disagreed that we figured out how it could happen. This was a real tribute to the NTSB staff."

On April 6, 2001, Bruce Morton of CNN aired a segment on Goglia's use of the assembled wreckage of TWA 800 as a kind of Long Island classroom. Over time, Goglia had brought hundreds of people to the facility that housed the assembled wreckage.

As Goglia was showing the CNN crew and a group of visitors, mostly aviation personnel, around, he said: "See the tags here? The red is particularly important because those are the first pieces to leave the airplane. And one of the clues we have in an accident is the first pieces to leave the airplane usually tell the story about what happened." Even though the plane had crashed into the Atlantic, its restoration was amazingly 97 percent complete. There were about a million pieces, and it took four years of meticulous lab work to put the immense puzzle together. It was soon to be moved from Long Island to Virginia, to continue to serve as a classroom for people in the aviation business.

In a personally revealing moment on the tour, Goglia said: "As a former mechanic, I can recall the feelings that I experienced after my first accident. And I still feel. That pain doesn't go away. Many of us in this room feel that over and over and over. It does take a toll on us."

Morton asked Goglia: "How do you make a difference?" Goglia replied: "By sharing what we know. You know, inside the NTSB, inside the FAA, inside the minds of a lot of good people, resides information that makes many of the accidents that I have to look at unnecessary. We need to get that information out."

Preacher and Teacher

"I'd often said the job at the NTSB was, at times, like being a preacher," Goglia told *Magis*. Indeed, much of Goglia's career has been that of preacher and teacher. His work as a teacher is illustrated by his unique Long Island classroom—the million-piece puzzle—and by his teaching lessons that can be learned from a terrible tragedy after exhausting efforts and deep study.

His preaching is not of the fire-and-brimstone variety, which consigns the wicked to a fiery pit for all eternity. Instead, his preaching is compassionate and hence, in the end, more compelling. People act in better ways because they want to act in better ways, not because they fear some judgment day. Often using examples from his own life, shared with uncommon candor, Goglia guides people toward ethical safety actions on the job. Like a preacher, he searches for instructive stories. Here is one of them.

As a young aviation mechanic, trying to learn everything, he went along with his superiors. By doing so, he points out, one can learn bad things as well as good. But, by the time he was confronted with an ethical question, he had gained some self-confidence. He had already served as shop steward—"the person who gets beat up by management above and union membership below. My wounds had already scabbed over and healed up." He fears that if the occasion in question had occurred earlier, he might not have had the self-confidence to do the right thing.

One day he was working the afternoon shift when a plane came in with "FOD"—foreign object debris, often debris picked up off the runway that passes through a jet engine, causing damage known as "tooth decay" to the turbine blades. After Goglia did the necessary mechanic's maintenance work on the aircraft, he called the out-of-town manager to tell him that the aircraft fell below the FOD safety standard. The manager told him to sign off on it anyway. In colorful language, Goglia told the manager that he had two choices: he could get on a plane and come up to Boston and sign off on it himself, or he could find someone else to do it—but Goglia wasn't going to do it. A half-hour later the local shift manager sauntered in and signed off on the plane.

When Goglia tells the story, the underlying message comes across clearly: he is not perfect, and if less seasoned he might have not been able to stand up to the manager. Luckily, finally, he got it right and stood tall; others backed off, and he felt better about himself. Of his action he says: "You don't have to do it that often. After a while people don't even bother you; they don't want the grief."

Goglia shares stories like that with young people coming up in the aviation industry, when speaking at aviation schools and before aviation maintenance groups, as a way to nudge them toward ethical behavior on the job. He knows you can improve aviation maintenance safety by improving the human factor, helping to shape a culture of safety, which is a best practice. This kind of preaching and teaching is one of the reasons why, in 2004, *Aviation Maintenance* renamed its annual "Time Out for Safety Award" the "John J. Goglia Time Out for Safety Award." The award recognizes those individuals who make a significant contribution to aviation maintenance safety.

When on the NTSB, Goglia actively pursued issues of aviation maintenance safety as only someone technically knowledgeable could do, even though that doubtless angered some of his former colleagues in aviation maintenance. He started harmlessly enough with a data request—asking the NTSB staff if they could give him the statistics on the percentage of accidents or incidents across time where maintenance was listed as a significant contributing factor. "I got this thousand-yard stare, you know, the glassy-eyed one, 'what are you talking about?'" he later told a group of aerospace engineers.

Using his own money, Goglia hired a Purdue student to come to Washington and painstakingly go through all the historical reports. The student came up with a figure of 16.9 percent, as opposed to the 3 percent to 5 percent that others, with no research to back their figures up, routinely used. In his mechanic's bones, Goglia had felt that the lower figures were too low, and he was right to go after real numbers. Doing so caused aviation maintenance to stand out more clearly as something that needed improving to better protect aircraft and air travelers.

One of the key issues Goglia raised while on the NTSB—and continues to raise—was the declining number of properly qualified and supervised mechanics doing maintenance on our commercial fleet of planes. He feels that this phenomenon must have a negative effect on the quality of maintenance done on those airplanes. Goglia's training was blue-chip: he was an FAA-certified A&P mechanic. But, after 9/11, when the airlines were suffering financially, the quality of airline maintenance began to diminish. Goglia told Lombardo: "All the airlines have broken their labor agreements in one form or another and are contracting out their heavy maintenance to FAR Part 145 Repair stations [stations certified under Part 145 of the federal aviation regulations]. The thing is that, if you're a repair station, you only need one A&P. Everyone else can work under that person's direction." The A&P mechanic is supposed to provide oversight, but Goglia discovered that at some repair stations, the ratio of A&P mechanic to noncertified mechanics was one to seven, one to eight, even one to nine—far too low for proper oversight. Airlines farm out maintenance work to repair stations to save money. At the time of Lombardo's 2004 article, non-A&P mechanics were earning $10 to $12 an hour, well below what a skilled A&P mechanic would work for. In classic style, Goglia pulled up a telling fact for Lombardo, doubtless garnered from his reading: "Disneyland has more A&Ps than anybody; they love that an A&P has pneumatic, hydraulic, and other industrial skills."

System Safety

In a nutshell, the work of the NTSB is determining the probable cause of accidents and recommending steps to prevent similar accidents from recurring. Yet types of accidents often do recur, which is the reason Goglia says there is nothing new in accidents, and virtually all accidents are preventable. Why do they recur?

Of his work on the NTSB, Goglia told Lombardo: "Going in, my focus was narrow. I was very focused on the task. . . . 'This task isn't right,' 'This paperwork isn't right,' that sort of thing. Now what I see is the problem really is the system. The problems I used to see still exist, but they're much bigger and broader than I imagined."

Goglia believes many good safety practices have already been developed; that is the good news. As he told Morton, "inside the minds of a lot of good people, resides information that makes many of the accidents that I have to look at unnecessary." The problem is that the good practices have not been linked in any systematic way; there is no integrated system for implementing them.

When Goglia served on the NTSB, he came to have a global view of what needs to be done to prevent accidents and, if they occur, to better prepare people for dealing with them. Essentially, the problem comes down to finding the collective will "to pull together best practices, to connect the dots," as he suggested to *Magis*. In effect he was speaking of a systemwide safety approach. To prevent transportation accidents, "all we need to do is have a pretty robust system that takes a look at the process, and we can prevent virtually all of them."

There is one loose end to tie up in Goglia's story: his meeting the one other person whose life's work was dramatically changed when the Electra fell out of the sky at sunset into Winthrop Harbor, Roxie Laybourne. At the time Goglia was sixteen, at home in East Boston. Laybourne was forty-nine, at work at the Smithsonian's Museum of Natural History, 442 miles away in Washington. They would meet thirty-five years after the crash.

The Feather Lady

Roxie Laybourne, known in Washington as the feather lady, worked for the Biological Survey at the Museum of Natural History for more than forty years before retiring. As mentioned above, it was she who positively identified the charred remains found in the Electra's engines as those of European starlings and launched the field of forensic ornithology.

Bill Adair wrote a remarkable piece about the world-renowned ornithologist, inventing a Latinate ornithological name for her: "Roxius Amazingus." He could as well have dubbed her "Roxius Sui Generis," one of a kind.

Amid the Smithsonian's collection of 650,000 bird specimens, some dating to the 1860s, Laybourne developed a surefire technique for microscopic identification of feathers, even for small, burned bits of feathers. Not long after joining the NTSB, Goglia met Laybourne.

It seems a pity that no snapshot exists of their meeting, more than three decades after the crash that altered the compass headings of their work—both striving to save lives of air travelers, both with important things to say about how to protect planes and people from bird strikes. But Goglia has a clear recollection of the meeting:

> After I tossed one of my first hand grenades on the bird issue, I got a call from Roxie Laybourne at the Smithsonian. I knew who she was, but she didn't know me. She said, "I'd like to talk to you." And I said, "I'll be right over." She was only walking distance [from the NTSB offices], a quarter-mile away at the Smithsonian. She showed me all of her drawers of birds and feathers. She was amazing.

The word *amazing* was used by Goglia and Adair for good reason. As Adair wrote in "Roxius Amazingus": "It's a rare bird who can create a whole new science, solve murders and make airplanes safer."

Goglia recalls that when he first met Laybourne, then eighty-five years old, she was passing on her lifelong knowledge and experience to her successor, Dr. Carla J. Dove, who today heads up the Smithsonian's feather lab. Even after Laybourne's retirement, she was frequently seen in the lab, helping others. The lab carries Laybourne's work forward, using her methods and increasingly the latest in DNA analysis to identify bird remains—especially since those Fedex and DHL packages arriving at the lab after bird strikes often contain only snarge.

After Laybourne's death in August 2003, at nearly ninety-three, Carla Dove, Marcy Heacker, and Bill Adair published a tribute to her life and work in the October 2004 issue of *The Auk*, the journal of the American Ornithologists' Union. They said of the Boston Electra crash: "That case became the cornerstone of Roxie's work on bird strike issues, which eventually led to the development of the first laboratory in the world dedicated solely to feather identification."

After Laybourne's findings in the Electra case, airport officials around the country finally began bird mitigation programs to discourage flocks of birds from gathering at their airports, basing their programs on science, particularly the behavior of the bird species that are the local problem. The officials began to take steps to make airports less hospitable to bird life, including mowing the grass on airport grounds and filling in wetlands. Airplane manufacturers improved jet engines, windscreens, and canopies to better withstand bird strikes. The U.S. Air Force, the FAA, the NTSB, and aircraft engine manufacturers like Rolls Royce and Pratt & Whitney all sought out Laybourne's expertise. On a trip to her home, Adair noticed hanging on the wall of her living room a plaque that honored her contribution to "A Study of Bird Ingestions into High-Bypass Ratio Turbine Aircraft Engines." Not every girl born in 1910 in Fayetteville, North Carolina, ended up with something like that on her wall.

Writing in *The New York Times* after Laybourne's passing, Anahad O'Connor encapsulated her work to help protect planes and air travelers from avian strike, following her role in the case of the Boston Electra:

> Over the next decades, Ms. Laybourne helped identify thousands of birds involved in collisions with commercial and military aircraft. Her work gave plane manufacturers information for designing engines that could continue to fly after ingesting the birds, and it helped ornithologists create bird management programs to prevent flocks from gathering near airports.

The techniques that Laybourne developed to identify feather remains were also used to help solve crimes of vandalism, poaching, kidnapping, and even murder. She testified in court cases as an expert witness. O'Connor noted: "In one homicide she matched the down in a pillow that was used to silence the murder weapon to traces of down found on the defendant's trouser cuff." In another case, Adair reported, Laybourne "helped the FBI catch a killer even though the victim's body had been dumped off a cliff into the ocean and couldn't be found. Roxie helped match goose feathers from the suspect's van with the victim's down coat." O'Connor offered a tribute from Doug Deedrick, a special agent at the FBI research lab at Quantico, Virginia, who had trained under Laybourne: "We depended upon her. . . . She was regarded as probably the foremost feather identification expert in the world."

In an obituary in *The Washington Post*, Louie Estrada described the technique Laybourne had developed for feather identification: "Her novel approach centered on careful analysis of barbules and other minute structural characteristics of feathers unique to different species." Often she worked with mere feather fragments, "some no bigger than bread crumbs," as Adair noted. She would slip the fragment under a trusty microscope issued her decades before by the then-new FAA and study the feather's microstructure—in effect, seeing a CSI-worthy fingerprint that allowed positive identification of the bird species. The FBI's use of "Roxie's science," as Adair dubbed it, appears in the mystery writer Patricia Cornwell's *Cruel and Unusual*.

Laybourne's outstanding scientific work of great practical use to society drew many dollars to the feather lab, with the U.S. Air Force providing general funding and now the FAA paying for a geneticist to identify birds using DNA analysis. Laybourne always made time to train younger scientists who wished to follow in her footsteps—like Dove and Heacker—who studied in what Adair called the "University of Roxie." Today, the contributions of the Feather Identification Laboratory are recognized globally. Indeed, in the acknowledgments of *The Man Who Flies with Birds*, set in Israel, half a world away, Vogel and Leshem thank Carla Dove and her staff at the Museum of Natural History for their help.

How did Laybourne become a world expert? The oldest of fifteen children, she was an independent spirit from the get-go. "Other girls growing up in the 1920s wanted to be nurses or teachers. Roxie wanted to be a turkey vulture," Adair wrote. "She would lie in the woods, watch them [the vultures] soar above the trees and dream of riding the thermals."

She earned a bachelor's degree from Meredith College in Raleigh,

North Carolina. The article about her in *The Auk* gives telling examples of her independent spirit, which later allowed her not only to arrive at the pinnacle of her field, but to create the field itself: "She was the first student at Meredith College to wear blue jeans and she once got in trouble for skipping classes to see Amelia Earhart arrive at a local airfield." Also at Meredith, she wanted to take an off-campus course in airplane engines, but college officials refused to give her permission, contending it would interfere with her school work. So she quietly took a correspondence course instead and got a part-time job working on airplane engines.

Decades later, Pratt & Whitney and other engine manufacturers would steadily ship bird remains to Laybourne from distant locations. Recognition of her many contributions over the years on the bird strike issue was evident to Adair when he visited her; in the living room he also saw "the elegant eagle statue that the Bird Strike Committee USA presented her, its Lifetime Achievement Award." After college, where she had majored in mathematics and general science, Laybourne earned a master's degree in botany from George Washington University. She joined the staff at the Smithsonian in 1944 on a temporary assignment that ended up lasting forty-four years.

What Laybourne and Goglia shared, beyond a connection to the Electra crash and lives devoted to protecting air travelers, is what got them to positions of high influence. Both had unquenchable curiosity, a desire to serve, and relentless passion for what they undertook. Which brings us full circle to the epigraph from Eudora Welty at the beginning of this chapter: "Passion is our ground, our island—do others exist?"

Not for John Goglia or Roxie Laybourne.

Epilogue: Mozart and the Starling

On May 27, 1784, Wolfgang Amadeus Mozart stepped into a shop and heard a starling whistling a theme from the final movement of his new piano concerto. He had finished the Piano Concerto no. 17 in G Major on April 12.

Few had heard the concerto by May 27, since he had kept it under wraps until its first performance, set for June 13. But so delighted was Mozart on hearing the starling's performance that he bought the bird as a pet, noting the details of the purchase in his expense diary: the date, the price, and, in musical notation, the theme the bird was whistling when he walked into the shop, adding "Das war schön!" (that was beautiful). The bird had whistled the theme perfectly, except for singing a G sharp where Mozart had written a G natural. Then again starlings in effect have two voice boxes: they are able to produce two different tunes simultaneously, even to sing duets with themselves, a feat that makes it easy enough to get mixed up.

How the starling learned the theme remains a mystery. Perhaps the student for whom the concerto was written wandered into the shop whistling the tune; perhaps Mozart, a known whistler, had been in the shop before. Starlings are supreme mimickers of sound.

In any case, the starling and Mozart were boon companions for three years until, sadly, the starling died. It is understandable that the musical genius and the mimicker would grow close. Of course, this was long before recording devices. If a composer wanted to hear his music played, somebody would have to perform it. Now Mozart could whistle a theme as he passed idly by the bird's cage, and hear it "played back" instantly from his gifted friend, the starling.

Mozart, sometimes odd and off-key in his personal life, touchingly arranged a full-fledged funeral for the bird, complete with veiled mourners, a graveside service, and a poem Mozart had written for the occasion and read aloud; his versification was no match for his genius as a composer. But the poem includes a sweet epitaph to his avian friend: "A little fool lies here / Whom I held dear." Mozart was using "fool" in the medieval sense of a jester, one who amuses his master or makes him laugh.

It is a fascinating story, a great musical genius and his dear friend —a bird weighing less than three ounces. Mozart could not know that one day the bird's species would become a dread threat to jetliners and cause the two worst aviation disasters triggered by bird strike in the first century of powered human flight.

Our relationship with birds is a complicated one, but we are inextricably entwined with them. Here we have a starling as a dear friend of Mozart, a composer of soaring imagination who, without benefit of powered flight still, in the words of the pilot-poet John Magee, "topped the wind-swept heights with easy grace" and "touched the face of God."

The story of Mozart's starling reminds us that, regardless of our field of endeavor, birds soaring in flight above us egg us ever onward, urging us to let our spirits fly.

As Carl Sandburg wrote, "Poetry is the journal of the sea animal, living on land, wanting to fly in the air." Over time we have handled that legacy of our lives and desires rather well. Surely we can share the skies of our dreams with birds, if we only try.

Acknowledgments

When I began to delve into the story of the Electra crash in Boston, I was driven by an inability to forget a story from my boyhood—of the day when a classmate walked into my meteorology and navigation class at Boston English High School and announced that he had spent the night before in scuba gear in Winthrop Harbor, searching for bodies after a plane crash. That was shocking news to me, a seventeen-year-old. The date was October 5, 1960. It turned out the plane had been knocked out of the sky by starlings. "How could that be?" I wondered.

Life took me many places before I returned to that story after retiring from Brandeis in 2002. I went back and began to read all the news stories of the time about the crash. There seemed to be so much information there, yet many questions remained. Each new place I looked for some answer led me to other places, with other questions and answers. Every satisfied curiosity led to a new perplexity. Eventually I probably came to know more about this story than anybody else, and I came to realize that, although the crash happened fifty years ago, it was tied to the danger today of catastrophic air disasters caused by bird strike.

The first opportunity I had to publish an article about the October 4, 1960, Electra crash was given me by Will Manus, a distinguished writer of many books, plays, and articles. A magnanimous spirit, fervently supportive of other writers, Will published my "Bird Strike" in the January–February 2008 issue of *Lively Arts*, his online cultural magazine, which focuses on the arts but includes human-interest stories.

The chance to turn the story into a full-length book came from the support of three people. I thank President Jehuda Reinharz of Brandeis University and Dr. John Hose, executive assistant to the president, for their belief in the project from the start. Dr. Phyllis Deutsch, editor in chief at the University Press of New England, saw a book in the slender 3,300-word article I sent her. I am deeply grateful to her and the UPNE Editorial Board for approving the book project. Phyllis also served as my editor during the writing process. We had worked together on a previous book, and I had learned then that Phyllis is smart, speedy, and always right. I also learned from the previous project that the staff at UPNE is uniformly terrific, rightfully proud of the high esteem in which the press is held, and living up to its high standards every day.

In the course of writing the book, I learned much about aviation, met fascinating people, and made a great friend in John Goglia. John had been a year behind me at English High, but I did not know him then. (My high school seems to have had a disproportionate share of boys present in Winthrop Harbor the night of the crash.) John became my guide and teacher, and what a gifted teacher he was—endlessly patient in explaining the intricacies of how jet engines work, how the nation's aviation system works, and how the National Transportation Safety Board operates amid Washington's political realities. It was when I was with John that I realized that Washington probably has the highest incidence of collisions between idealism and reality of any city in the world.

But let me list other treasured helpers, without whose aid I would have faltered. My friend of many years, Richard Daggett, arranged for me to meet with his son-in-law, Lieutenant Colonel Sean Mooney of the New Hampshire Air National Guard, a captain and career pilot who shared with me his superb flying sense, his experience as a pilot, and his rich knowledge of what happens in a cockpit, a place foreign to me. His joy in talking about flying was inspirational. He gave me invaluable information about the latest technologies that military pilots can use when planning flights, so as to try to avoid routes or times of day when there will be high concentrations of birds.

My nephew, Mark Kalafatas, a polymath who is at once an aeronautical engineer, a lawyer, a chess master, and the holder of an advanced degree in U.S. history, kindly read the aeronautical engineering passages to ensure their accuracy. Any inaccuracies that might now appear are solely the doing of his less talented uncle.

My longtime, wonderful physician, Dr. Peter Gross of the Massachusetts General Hospital, put me in touch with Dr. Earle W. Wilkins, for twenty years the chief of Emergency Medical Services at MGH, who explained to me what Boston's medical response to disaster was like in the era of the Electra crash, and described his struggle to create the highly coordinated, citywide medical response to disaster that now exists. Dr. Wilkins is ninety years old, and after a half-hour's conversation with him, trying to keep up with his quick mind, I was sweating profusely.

I want to thank Kim Nix and the sweet staff of the Wadsworth Library at Mt. Ida College in Newton, Massachusetts, for so generously renewing Robert Serling's *The Electra Story* ten times. Surely that is a library record. I also want to thank Aaron Schmidt at the Boston Public Library, Dr. Carla Dove and Ellen Alers at the Smithsonian Institution, and Sue Hardy for securing wonderful archival photographs.

Others who added a critical piece of information, an insight, or put me onto something valuable that made the book better include Ellen T. Delaney, Jackie Greene, Bill Hollick, John and Fran Kreinces, Liliana Leombruno, Adam Libert, Fred and Judy Luddy, John Luddy, George Murphy, Marjorie Rosenbaum, Mike Seltz, Joe Sieber, Ira Steinberg, Margaret Sullivan, Tracy Tully, and Steve Wagner.

I want to thank Susan Simon, my dear friend and admissions colleague across decades—first at Brandeis and now at her college counseling firm, Admissions Advantage—for her kind support and understanding as I skittered between work on this book and counseling young people.

Above all there is my family: John and Karen Kalafatas, and Dan Kalafatas and Hadley Mullin, who have played a larger part and helped more than they can know with their loving support and encouragement; and my wife, Joan, who has been an unfailing inspiration with her clarity of mind, editorial skills, and devotion. Each time dark clouds passed overhead, she was there, as always in my life, a bright morning star to light the way. Without her there would be no book.

And I want to thank my father, a skilled machinist and tool-and-die maker at General Electric's Aircraft Division in Lynn, Massachusetts, in the late 1940s and 1950s. He was so spectacular at what he did that no one at GE seemed to care that he was a leftist rabble-rouser. One special day, when GE invited employees to bring in their families to see the workplace, he brought me, then nine years old, to see the J-47 Sabre Jet engine he was working on. I loved Sabre Jets and built models of them at home as he worked on the real engines in Lynn. I marveled at the many highly polished, glinting turbine blades that helped power the plane to six consecutive world airspeed records. I think that standing with him, next to the impressive machine that he had touched with his always careful, craftsman's hands, talismanically led to this book. My father passed away long ago, but as I wrote this book, I kept before me on my desk his GE badge and picture. Thanks, Dad!

Vital Statistics of the Boston Electra

Lockheed L-188 Electra N5533

Manufacturing completed: June 8, 1959

U.S. registry number: N5533

Length: 104 feet, 6 inches

Wingspan: 99 feet

Maximum takeoff weight: 113,000 pounds

Fuel capacity: 5,520 gallons

Engines: Allison 501-D13

Maximum speed: 448 miles per hour

Maximum altitude: 28,400 feet

Net weight: 60,000 pounds

Cost: $2,500,000

Line number: 62 (62nd of 170 Electras built)

Miles flown: 1 million

Time flown: 3,561 hours, 29 minutes

Passengers carried: 88,000

Number of propellers changed: 11

Number of engines changed: 12

Major overhauls: 17; final overhaul, 5 flying hours before last flight

Bomb scares: 1 (turned back on a flight from Miami to St. Louis; inspected, no bomb found)

Next to last flight: New York to Boston (normal)

Flight 375 baggage weight: 840 pounds

Flight 375 passenger weight: 10,720 pounds

Source: Compiled from Upton, *Lockheed L-188 Electra*; and Friendly, "CBS Reports: The Case of the Boston Electra."

Select Bibliography

Below are some of the sources I turned to in writing this book. The list is not meant to be a complete one, but rather to give the reader a feel for the range and variety of materials consulted and to offer some convenient leads to anyone wishing to study further the matters raised in this book. Many of the organizations mentioned in the book—such as the Bird Strike Committee USA, the Federal Aviation Administration, the National Audubon Society, the National Transportation Safety Board, and Transport Canada—have well-developed, helpful websites easily found via any search engine.

Adair, Bill. "For Aviation Investigator, Every Crash Hurts." *St. Petersburg Times*, March 23, 2004.

————. "Roxius Amazingus." *St. Petersburg Times*, November 21, 1999.

Alexander, Paul. *Rough Magic: A Biography of Sylvia Plath*. Paperback ed. Cambridge, Mass.: Da Capo Press, 2003.

Associate Administrator of Airports, Office of Airport Safety and Standards. "Wildlife Strikes to Civil Aircraft in the United States, 1990–2008." Federal Aviation Administration National Wildlife Strike Database Serial Report 15. September 2009. Available online at http://wildlife.pr.erau.edu/BASH90-08.pdf.

Barcott, Bruce. "Clearing the Air." *Audubon*, June 2009, 73–76.

Boston Globe. Coverage of the Boston Electra crash. October 5–8, 1960.

Civil Aeronautics Board. *Accident Report: Eastern Air Lines, Inc., Lockheed Electra L-188 N5533, Logan International Airport, Boston, MA, October 4, 1960*. Department of Transportation Library File No. 1–0043. Washington: Civil Aeronautics Board, July 31, 1962.

Dolbeer, Richard A., and Paul Eschenfelder. "Have Population Increases of Large Birds Outpaced Airworthiness Standards for Civil Aircraft?" USDA National Wildlife Research Center Staff Publications, 2002. Available online at http://digitalcommons.unl.edu/icwdm_usdanwrc/477.

Friendly, Fred W. "CBS Reports: The Case of the Boston Electra." February 16, 1961.

"John Goglia Is a Man on a Mission," *Magis* (Parks College of Engineering, Aviation and Technology, Saint Louis University), Spring 2005, 5–9.

Lombardo, David A. "John Goglia, a Rebel with a Cause, Reflects on NTSB Tenure." *AINonline*, July 2004. Available online at http://www.ainonline.com.

Mackinnon, Bruce, Richard Sowden, Kristi Russell, and Stewart Dudley, eds. *Sharing the Skies: An Aviation Industry Guide to the Management of Wildlife Hazards*. 2nd ed. Ottawa: Transport Canada, 2001.

Mahler, Donald. "The Plane Exploded on Impact," "At Crash Site, Devastation," and "Lives Changed Forever." *Valley News* (West Lebanon, N.H.), October 25–27, 2008.

Murphy, George. "Electra or the Birds of Death and the Mongoloid Troubadour: A Monologue." Performed by George Murphy at the Red Barn Theatre, Key West, Florida, January 6, 7, 13, and 14, 2008.

Serling, Robert J. *The Electra Story: The Dramatic History of Aviation's Most Controversial Airliner*. Garden City, N.Y.: Doubleday, 1963.

Serling, Robert J., and the editors of Time-Life Books. *The Jet Age*. Alexandria, Va.: Time-Life Books, 1982.

Upton, Jim. *Lockheed L-188 Electra*. Airliner Tech Series 5. North Branch, Minn.: Specialty Press Publishers and Wholesalers, 1999.

Vogel, Carole Garbuny, and Yossi Leshem. *The Man Who Flies with Birds*. Minneapolis: Kar-Ben Publishing, 2009.

West, Meredith J., and Andrew P. King. "Mozart's Starling." *American Scientist* 78 (May–June 1990): 106–14. Available online at http://www.starlingtalk.com/mozart1.htm.